Prepare for the Great Tribulation and the Era of Peace

Prepare for the Great Tribulation and the Era of Peace

Volume VI:
January 1, 1997 – March 31, 1997

by John Leary

PUBLISHING COMPANY
P.O Box 42028 Santa Barbara, CA 93140-2028
(800) 647-9882 • (805) 957-4893 • Fax: (805) 957-1631

The publisher recognizes and accepts that the final authority regarding these apparitions and messages rests with the Holy See of Rome, to whose judgement we willingly submit.

– The Publisher

Cover art by Josyp Terelya

©1997 Queenship Publishing

Library of Congress Number #

Published by:
   Queenship Publishing
   P.O. Box 42028
   Santa Barbara, CA 93140-2028
   (800) 647-9882 • (805) 957-4893 • Fax: (805) 957-1631

Printed in the United States of America

ISBN: 1-57918-002-7

Acknowledgments

It is in a spirit of deep gratitude that I would like to acknowledge first the Holy Trinity: Father, Jesus, and the Holy Spirit, the Blessed Virgin Mary and the many saints and angels who have made this book possible.

My wife, Carol, has been an invaluable partner. Her complete support of faith and prayers has allowed us to work as a team. This was especially true in the many hours of indexing and proofing of the manuscript. All of our family has been a source of care and support.

I am greatly indebted to Josyp Terelya for his very gracious offer to provide the art work for this publication. He has spent three months of work and prayer to provide us with a selection of many original pictures. He wanted very much to enhance the visions and messages with these beautiful and provocative works. You will experience some of them throughout these volumes.

A very special thank you goes to my spiritual director, Fr. Leo J. Klem, C.S.B. No matter what hour I called him, he was always there with his confident wisdom, guidance and discernment. His love, humility, deep faith and trust are a true inspiration.

My appreciation also goes to Father John V. Rosse, my good pastor at Holy Name of Jesus Church. He has been open, loving and supportive from the very beginning.

There are many friends and relatives whose interest, love and prayerful support have been a real gift from God. Our own Wednesday, Monday and First Saturday prayer groups deserve a special thank you for their loyalty and faithfulness.

Finally, I would like to thank Bob and Claire Schaefer of Queenship Publishing for providing the opportunity to bring this message of preparation, love and warnings to you the people of God.

John Leary, Jr.

Dedication

To the Most Holy Trinity

God

The Father, Son and Holy Spirit

The Source of

All

Life, Love and Wisdom

Publisher's Foreword

John has, with some exceptions, been having visions twice a day since they began in July, 1993. The first vision of the day usually takes place during morning Mass, immediately after he receives the Eucharist. If the name of the church is not mentioned, it is a local Rochester, NY, church. When out of town, the church name is included in the text. The second vision occurs in the evening, either at Perpetual Adoration or at the prayer group that is held at Holy Name of Jesus Church.

Various names appear in the text. Most of the time, the names appear only once or twice. Their identity is not important to the message and their reason for being in the text is evident First names have been used, when requested by the individual. The name Maria E., which occurs quite often, is the visionary Maria Esperanza Bianchini of Betania, Venezuela.

We are grateful to Josep Terelya for the cover art, as well as for the art throughout the book. Josyp is a well-known visionary and also, the author of *Witness* and most recently *In the Kingdom of the Spirit.*

This volume covers visions from January 1, 1997 through March 31, 1997. The volumes will now be coming out quarterly due to the urgency of the messages. Volume I contains visions from July, 1993 through June, 1994. Volume II contains visions from July, 1994 through June, 1995. Volume III contains visions from July, 1995 through July 10, 1996. Volume IV contains visions from July, 11 1996 through September 30, 1996. Volume V contains visions from October 1, 1996 through December 31, 1996

The Publisher

Foreword

It was in July of 1993 that Almighty God, especially through Jesus, His Eternal Word, entered the life of John Leary in a most remarkable way. John is 54 years old and works as a chemist at Eastman Kodak Co., Rochester, New York. He lives in a modest house in the suburbs of Rochester with Carol, his wife of thirty-one years, and Catherine, his youngest daughter. His other two daughters, Jeanette and Donna, are married and have homes of their own. John has been going to daily Mass since he was seventeen and has been conducting a weekly prayer group in his own home for twenty-five years. For a long time, he has been saying fifteen decades of the Rosary each day.

In April of 1993 he and his wife made a pilgrimage to Our Lady's shrine in Medjugorje, Yugoslavia. While there, he felt a special attraction to Jesus in the Blessed Sacrament. There he became aware that the Lord Jesus was asking him to change his way of life and to make Him his first priority. A month later in his home, Our Lord spoke to him and asked if he would give over his will to Him to bring about a very special mission. Without knowing clearly to what he was consenting, John, strong in faith and trust, agreed to all the Lord would ask.

On July 21, 1993 the Lord gave him an inkling of what would be involved in this new calling. He was returning home from Toronto in Canada where he had listened to a talk of Maria Esperanza (a visionary from Betania, Venezuela) and had visited Josyp Terelya. While in bed, he had a mysterious interior vision of a newspaper headline that spelled "DISASTER." Thus began a series of daily and often twice daily interior visions along with messages, mostly from Jesus. Other messages were from God the Father, the Holy Spirit, the Blessed Virgin Mary, his guardian angel and many of the saints, especially St. Therese of Lisieux. These messages he recorded on his word processor. In the beginning, they were quite short, but they became more extensive as the weeks passed by. At the time of this writing, he is still receiving visions and messages.

These daily spiritual experiences, which occur most often immediately following Communion, consist of a brief vision which becomes the basis of the message that follows. They range widely on a great variety of subjects, but one might group them under the following categories: warnings, teachings and love messages. Occasionally, there are personal confirmations of some special requests that he made to the Lord.

The interior visions contain an amazing number of different pictures, some quite startling, which hardly repeat themselves. In regard to the explicit messages that are inspired by each vision, they contain deep insights into the kind of relationship God wishes to establish with His human creatures. There, also, is an awareness of how much He loves us and yearns for our response. As a great saint once wrote: "Love is repaid only by love." On the other hand, God is not a fool to be treated lightly. In fact, did not Jesus once say something about not casting pearls before the swine? Thus, there are certain warnings addressed to those who shrug God off as if He did not exist or is not important in human life.

Along with such warnings, we become more conscious of the reality of Satan and the forces of evil "...which wander through the world seeking the ruin of souls." We used to recite this at the end of each low Mass. In His love and concern for us, Our Lord keeps constantly pointing out how frail we humans are in the face of such evil angelic powers. God is speaking of the necessity of daily prayer, of personal penance, and of turning away from atheistic and material enticements which are so much a part of our modern environment.

Perhaps the most controversial parts of the messages are those which deal with what we commonly call Apocalyptic. Unusual as these may be, in my judgment, they are not basically any different than what we find in the last book of the New Testament or in some of the writings of St. Paul. After a careful and prayerful reading of the hundreds of pages in this book, I have not found anything contrary to the authentic teaching authority of the Roman Catholic Church.

The 16th Century Spanish mystic, St. John of the Cross, gives us sound guidelines for discerning the authenticity of this sort of phenomenon involving visions, locutions, etc. According to him, there are three possible sources: the devil, some kind of self-imposed hypnosis or God. I have been John's spiritual confidant for over three years. I have tested him in various spiritual ways and I am most confident that all he has put into these messages is neither of the devil nor of some kind of mental illness. Rather, they are from the God who, in His love for us, wishes to reveal His own Divine mind and heart. He has used John for this. I know that John is quite ready to abide by any decision of proper ecclesiastical authority on what he has written in this book

Rev. Leo J. Klem, C.S.B.
Rochester, New York

Visions and Messages
of John Leary:

Wednesday, January 1, 1997: (Solemnity of Mary)
After Communion, I could see some plates and other things about home. Then I saw a beautiful earth followed by a brief glimpse of an emotionally loving bright light from Heaven. Jesus said: *"My people, many get nostalgic when they talk about coming back to the home of their youth. But rather than dwell on just an earthly home, think of the real home I am calling you to, both on earth in the era of peace and your final home in heaven. Keep these thoughts ever in your heart and focused on Me who leads you there. Those, who love Me sincerely and follow My Will, can look forward to this heavenly reward. Even more, you can begin trying to live in My Divine Will in preparation for how your life will be with Me. Think to give Me praise and thanks each day, much like you will be doing after My purification of the earth. I come to bring all of My children home to Me, but you must return My love and work on your spiritual perfection each day. It is the intention of the love in your heart, that I look for in everyone. I know you all have failings, but if it is your purpose to seek forgiveness and right your life with Me, that is what I will reward you for."*

Thursday, January 2, 1997:
After Communion, I was looking down a road and it had shaded portions and sunlit areas. Jesus said: *"My people, each person looks down the highway of life with your own individual trials and joys. It is good that you share with one another to get through these trials. You are all tested in faith in various ways, but never beyond your endurance by My graces. Comfort those in sick-*

ness or in grief of the dying, for everyone has their turn in this process of life. Keep strong in faith in Me and I will carry you through any difficulties. Those, who persevere in faith all their lives, will see life in the comfort of My arms. Others, who oppose Me, may find grief without any support. You may feel a hell on earth, if you do not seek My help. Everyone must face trials in their lives, but it is with faith that I will bring you through to the joy of My reward in heaven."

Later, at the prayer group, in Church, I saw a tall flame and a chariot which was a reminder of how the angel of fire protected the Hebrews from the Egyptian soldiers. Jesus said: *"My people, you are seeing how I protected My chosen people with a pillar of fire from the Egyptian army in the Exodus. As I protected My people in those days, so you will see My miraculous protection come over My faithful remnant. Those, who pray and trust in Me, will be watched over throughout the whole tribulation. Bear with time, for it will be short in duration during this trial. You will see fright-ful, evil events, but for the sake of the elect, this time will be short-ened."* I could see Our Lady come and there were barbed wire fences in front of her. Mary said: *"My dear children, I come as a Mother of Peace seeking to stop the fighting among my children. My Son came to give peace and rest to the earth, but they would not accept His Word, because it would change their comfortable lives. Listen to my Son's words and treasure them in your heart as I did. No matter what comes against you, call on me and I will have my Son come to your rescue."* I could see some people in lines to get food from some foodshelves. Workers were handing out meals for a large crowd that did not have food. Jesus said: *"My people, as disasters and food shortages begin to plague your country, do not hide from your duty to help those in need of meals. Whenever you feed the hungry, you are helping Me. Be ready to do corporal acts of mercy for your neighbor, no matter what the circumstances may be. You, yourselves may require help in the future for food. Others may help you then, as they reach out their arms to feed you.* I could see some monks praying over the people. Jesus said: *"My people, many have gone before you to preserve the faith in their writings and their speech. These doctors of My Church have fought various heresies in their day. Even today, there are still false witnesses who doubt either My humanity or My Divinity. My evangelists of today must speak out in preserving the traditions of the faith. Look to My Pope son, John Paul II to lead you in faith and morals. Guard My Real Presence in the Eucharist and continue to give Me praise where My Host is in adoration. For those, who lead others to Me, you will receive a prophet's reward."* I could see an angel and there were beacons of light coming from his eyes. I asked Jesus for permission of my guardian angel, Mark, to speak. He said: *"My son, as you approach the time of the trial, call on me to help you in all of your problems. As you go out to evangelize, call on me to protect you from any attacks of the demons, who do not want you to save souls. Preach Christ crucified in your every day experiences, so all can draw on Jesus's most precious Blood to fight evil in their work. Angels will be more powerful now to help you in this evil age. Seek me and I will come to your aid. Do not forget that I am here to help you, but we cannot violate your free will unless you ask us to come."* I could see various people speaking at a conference. Jesus said: *"My son, you will see many are hungry for My Words of comfort and instruction. I am sending many of My messengers to go forward at this time to witness to the coming purification. Do not be afraid to go forward when I call you to witness to My messages. Many are yearning for My Sacred Presence, but they need help and encouragement in breaking their bonds of sin. Go preach to all nations, as I have commanded all of you to do."* I could see some spotlights shining down. Jesus said: *"My son, you are being called forward to go before many people to teach them in preparation for this tribulation. Do not fear any problems or personal cares in going forth to the places I call you. Keep sincere and humble in your daily prayers. Give Me all the praise in My messages and healings. Do not be tempted by any fame, but keep true to the responsibility of the mission I have given you. Seek the protection of your angel and the Holy Spirit in your speech."*

Friday, January 3, 1997:

After Communion, I could look up to the sky through the fields. There were ominous storms and signs. Jesus said: *"My people, I have told you many times that you are nearing the time of purification. Your storms will increase and continue to set records. Many will realize this year more than ever, that your weather is no longer normal. The one world people will continue to influence your weather even worse than before. As you look to the skies, you will see great signs of the Antichrist's coming. The signs, you see this year, will be the most significant to date. I have been spiritually preparing you to face the evil which will soon befall you. Take courage, My children, for I am beside you to protect you. Be prepared to be stripped of all you have, so you can flee away from the evil people who will be seeking you. Again, have your holy weapons and some essentials packed and ready to leave at a moment's notice."*

Later, I could see a spinning pinwheel and then some buses were traveling down the road. Jesus said: *"My people, this again is a sign of My warning, which is coming soon. This is not anything you can prevent or prepare for. I only have told you to keep your soul clean from mortal sin, since those people with serious sin will experience a deeper pain to see how such sin severs our love relationship. Those in such a state should seek a confessional to renew My love in their hearts and souls. Do not put off your monthly confession, but be vigilant in repenting of your sins. Those, who experience the warning, will have a deep remorse for how they have offended Me throughout their lives. This truly will be My last wake up call to many far away from Me. If these souls still fail to seek My forgiveness, their decision may seal their fate in everlasting hell. Help those after the warning to see the light and make amends with their Lord. You may not have much longer to share My mercy, when the evil one may come to steal these weak souls away from Me. Be on guard and protect your souls from all attacks of the evil one."*

Saturday, January 4, 1997:

After Communion, I could see an altar deep in some rocks where Mass was being offered. Jesus said: *"My people, I love you dearly and I am showing you how My Remnant Church will have to be in hiding in the future. I am asking you to remain close to the teachings of My Church as My Pope son, John Paul II, will lead My Remnant Church. Read My Scriptures daily, so you can be attentive to My Words. My Words of the Gospel show you the way to your salvation. Do not be misled by the false witnesses who will come to try and steal away even My elect. I am sending you My messengers at this time to help guide the people in shepherding My lambs from the evil men and evil spirits of this age. As your persecution begins, you will have to pray to Me and My angels who will lead you to safety. Whatever evil will confront you, I will be standing by your side to protect you and guide your speech."*

Sunday, January 5, 1997: (Epiphany)

At St. Paul the Apostle Church at Annville, Pa., after Communion, I could see a cup with the Host above it. Jesus said: *"My people, I greet you today as I feed you with the Bread of Kings in My Body and Blood. When you receive Me in Communion, you are at My Heavenly Banquet, which I invite you to at every Mass. As you celebrate the gifts from these kings of the orient, I am looking for you also to present your heavenly gifts to Me. Earthly gifts I appreciate that are given from the heart, but the real treasure, that you can give Me, are your spiritual gifts. When you offer your prayers, your works of mercy, and even your spirit in doing My Will, these are most precious in My eyes. I am King of the Universe and I come, so that your sins may be forgiven. Give praise and glory to God for all the many gifts I have bestowed upon you. If you can make the time today, especially come in adoration of My Blessed Sacrament, so I may dwell in your hearts and shine My love upon you."*

Later, I could see a creche scene made out of simple clay pottery. Jesus said: *"My people, I am asking you to come to Me at My crib as a simple, innocent child. Do not think you must come to Me with sophisticated prayers, or in many volumes of prayers. Just come as you are, where you are, with a humble and contrite heart. I await all of My children to seek My forgiveness in confession. Pray to Me from your heart, so that I can see you are sincere in your love for Me. I am a jealous God, since I wish all of My creatures would give Me reverence, praise and glory, as I deserve for creating you. If I did not will you into existence and maintain your being through the Holy Spirit, you literally would be nothing. When you give Me thanks for all I do for you, you are admitting My supremacy over all of mankind. Today is a feast of My Kingship. Continue to honor Me in adoration and give Me your witness of faith by following My Will for you. Thank you for spending this hour with Me and for your evangelical efforts as well."*

Monday, January 6, 1997:

After Communion, I could see a hat and it was overflowing with water. Jesus said: *"My people, I have shown you visions of the cup of My wrath overflowing. What you are seeing today is a hat overflowing, since men are now perpetrating disasters by enhancing weather patterns for their own use. Over these latest years, has it occurred to you why you are setting so many records in severe storms? Some has been a chastisement for your abortions, but men of the one world government are causing even worse destruction. Man has delved into areas of electronic and nuclear science that he does not even realize some of the consequences of his actions. If enough of these storms continue, you could see another tool of evil being used to bring you to your knees and make you ripe for takeover. Already massive areas of the northwest have been declared disaster areas. Such a scale of disasters could wipe out any insurance or federal aid. The next step is martial rule and a declaration of dictatorial powers over your constitutional rights."*

Later, I could see a pit of red. Then I rose up among some red skyscrapers to see that I was rising above a major city. Jesus said: *"My people, you are seeing this vision as an example of the filth and stench of sin that rises high to heaven in witness to your evil age. I ask you to pray for those especially in your cities where drugs, prostitution, abortion and many killings are going on. Your cities have become so corrupt, that many will find it hard to raise themselves up. It is greed and lust for money and earthly pleasures that motivate many in your cities. There are sinners in the rural areas, but not as bad as in the cities. This is why I tell you, you will soon have to flee your cities, as the persecution of My faithful begins. Wake up! My people of America, come to Me on bended knees; or you may die in your sins, when My justice condemns you. This is the time for your conversion, or you may never see Me again except at the final judgment. There, I will tell the accursed to be out of My sight and go to your eternal punishment. The lambs of My faithful, I will put over My shoulder and I will carry you into heaven to enjoy your eternal reward with Me."*

Tuesday, January 7, 1997:
After Communion, I could see a great light and glitter shining out from a valuable pearl. Jesus said: *"My people, My Kingdom is so valuable that it is like a man who would go out and sell all that he has to own it. Your faith in Me is also like a valuable pearl that no one would ever give up for any price. So when you see the worldly things around you, think more of the value of your faith and your salvation with Me in heaven. To reach your goal, to be with Me, you must strive every day to do My Will and fulfill the plan I have for your lives. Seek Me first and all else will be given you. Know that it is My unconditional love that is forever seeking you. Give into My divine pleasure by giving Me your love freely, by your own free will."*

Later, I could see some wrapped Christmas gifts and someone was getting into a car. Jesus said: *"My son, you have indeed been obedient to the mission I have given you. As you see, those that are willing to do My work, will not be lacking in things to do. You do need to pace yourself, but rest assured I will be helping you to fulfill all of My plans. You can detect there is a sense of urgency in your travels, since these opportunities will be coming to a close. As you approach the beginning of these happenings as foretold in the omens in the sky, your movements will not be so easy. You have seen the gifts that you have laid at My crib by your attendance at My calling. The car also indicates your traveling, but keep a humble, sincere spirit wherever you witness to My messages. You are being graced with this ministry, but it is your responsibility to carry out My Will for you. Do not be afraid to speak out wherever you go. Pray for My help and safety in visiting My children with My message. Many conversions and healings will come by Me, through you, but continue to give Me all the glory."*

Wednesday, January 8, 1997:

After Communion, I could see a dugout stone area ready for a funeral. Jesus said: *"My people, I am a God of the living and not the dead. He who has life in Me will be in eternity with Me. You must see the devil's hand in encouraging death. I have told you many times that it is the taking of life in abortion, suicide, or killing that I detest the most. In this case of assisted suicide, I am asking all of My faithful to reject the state's taking of life. This is another encroachment upon the preciousness of life as in abortion and euthanasia. Protect life in ALL of its forms. Some may obtain their purgatory on earth by suffering an agonizing death. I am the one to give and take life, so do not cease a life for which I have a plan. Those, who concur in such killing, will have to answer to Me at the judgment. So love one another and assist each other, but continue your fight against this death culture of Satan."*

Note: Vote near on Dr. Quill case in the Supreme Court on assisted suicide.

Thursday, January 9, 1997:

After Communion, I could see a vague image of Maria E. Then I saw a vision of a package of cheese in a white wrapping and it was laying in a wicker basket. Jesus said: *"My people, you are seeing in the basket only one package of cheese. This again is an indication to you of the coming famine. Food will become VERY difficult to find and only a few things will you be able to buy. Your weather problems will continue to make it difficult for farmers to provide enough food. As you see prices continue to rise, you will soon be advised of these shortages. This is why I have continued to ask you to set aside some food to provide during these shortages, for those in dire need and in deep prayer I will multiply what little they have. I love you so much, and I will watch over My little ones with a father's hand. Have faith in Me and I will provide for all of your needs, both physical and spiritual."*

Later, at the prayer group, I could see many angels of God coming like the angels that led the shepherds. Jesus said: *"My people, many times I have sent My angels as messengers and guides for travel. Look to the scriptures. Read how My angels led My people in the desert and how they led Lot and his family out of Sodom. When you see these things, is it any different in the time of the tribulation, that My angels will be called on to lead you to safety? As St. Joseph was awakened in the night and led to Egypt, so you also will be led into hiding. Do not fear, but have faith in My protection, for My love knows no bounds."* I could see an eagle representing the United States and he was being attacked by a demon. Jesus said: *"My people of America, why are you so blind to the demons who are trying to choke the spiritual life out of your country? You give Me lip service, but many are far from Me. You fail to see how your country's greatness came because of your faith in Me. If you continue to turn your back on Me, only death CAN come to your country. As the tribulation approaches, you soon will no longer recognize your government, as world powers will control you. Pray, My people, to accept the destiny you have called on yourselves. Only My purification will restore peace and love once again."* I could see a little child place a star at the foot of a bed. I asked if David's spirit could speak to me. David said: *"I am here again to greet my family as an intercessor in prayer for you. Please invite me into your lives to help where I can. I am watching over my sister and let her know that I am praying for her."* I could see some green lights going up into the heavens and the word 'HAARP' (High Frequency Active Auraral Research Project) flashed in front of me. Jesus said: *"My people, seek to stop these men who are experimenting with these weather making machines. Funds from your own country are aiding the one world government's plan to cause havoc in your weather. See that these evil uses of such machines will give the Antichrist a means of controlling your food making ability. This is a hard message, but you should know the evil designs that these men will strive to cause emergency powers to be invoked. Pray, My people, as you will be experiencing a*

9

vast struggle for power in controlling food and jobs." I could see Mary come with an image of Guadaloupe. Mary said: *"Pray, my dear children, for all those Lambs who are going forward to fight the wolves of your pro-abortion foes. Many of my confused children do not understand the lives that are at stake in the blood money being made on the dead babies. They have compounded their lust to control life and death, with their greed for money as well. Pray for those willing to fight this abortion mentality. If you pray enough, these places of abortions can be closed."* I could see some body bags in a dark room and President Clinton's face was shown. Jesus said: *"My people, this is a hard message for you to understand now, but in the future it will be commonplace. Power corrupts completely. Evil men are controlling your government, as they will be systematically removing all opposition to their plans for dictatorial control in your country. All those in their way will be gradually liquidated as has been done in some of your president's past experiences. Prepare for this as another reason to go into hiding."* I could see some lights on the ceiling in a hospital with machines all around. Jesus said: *"My people, as you approach the time of the Antichrist, know that evil men will use various means to control people's minds. At first it will be done subtly, but gradually the suggestions will become stronger. It will be an increasing brainwash of world control that will be forced on the people. These days of the tribulation are why I am sending you into hiding to protect you from losing your faith through such deceit. Pray for My help and I will protect you."*

Friday, January 10, 1997:

After Communion, I could see plenty of snow and some people cross country skiing. Jesus said: *"My people, your snow season is beginning in severe cold. You will continue to see more records for snow and cold this year. Your weather patterns are changing with a more severe twist. Many will be suffering hardships, so helping your neighbor more may be required of all. Here you may see hard times that might wake up some people in their spiritual complacency. Come alive in the faith and follow Me through whatever purification I send you. Many need to be shaken out of their earthly habits, so they can see that all does not revolve around the worldly pleasures. See during the dark days of winter there is an opportunity to be more prayerful. You may find yourself with more time inside, so use your time wisely to reform your lives in contemplation."*

Later, I could see a dark river of water and then a falls with a larger flow than usual. Jesus said: *"My people, you are being severely tested by water, snow and cold winds this winter. You would do well to store some extra food for times when you may not get to the store. In some areas travel is being restricted by cold winds, and in other areas floods are destroying the roads. You will see increasing damage with no way to start over for some. In all of these events, see this as a sign of My Second Coming. You will be purified of the worldly things and you will see that trust in Me is all that you have. Do not worry about dates of events, but let these things cause you to prepare yourself spiritually, as in confession. Your time for conversion grows short, so heed My call to get your life in order. Tell others in your travels of this same request. It is only by your perseverance in prayer and following My will, that you will win your salvation through Me."*

Saturday, January 11, 1997:

After Communion, I could see a flat truck where there were black handles to hold and stand by. Jesus said: *"My people, this black carrier represents the dark days of the coming purification. You are being shown these handles to hang on to in order for My messengers to show you how to hold on during this time. There will be much persecution for those believing in Me, but I will be protecting My lambs from being abused. Have faith that I will lead you to safety, but you will have to suffer much during this time. All you have, will be stripped from you, but then you will appreciate that your real treasure is being with Me. Pray for the sinners who are away from Me, since their souls carry a heavy price."*

Later, I saw some firemen coming down a pole in an emergency. I then saw a spectacular panorama with a circling cesspool of evil and a light in the middle. Jesus said: *"My people, I ask you to look around at your society and notice what is important to people. Many are so taken up with worldly concerns, that few think much of Me beyond Sunday. Is it any wonder that there is so much evil in your world, when little thought is given to a good spiritual life? Truly you are mingling in a cesspool of evil, but few even recognize the extent of evil about you. My children, My warning and My purification must come, since man will soon have no faith in Me. The evil one has so clouded your good intentions with the cares of the world, that you make little or no time for Me each day. My love is overflowing for you, but My justice demands repentance of your sins. I have a faithful remnant that is obedient to My Word. It is these few souls that are holding back the wrath of My hands. Continue fighting this battle against evil for My sake and your soul will be saved."*

Sunday, January 12, 1997:

At St. Joseph's Church, Binghamton, N.Y., after Communion, I could see someone drowning and a rope was let down to pull them out. Jesus said: *"My people, as you celebrate My Baptism, may you stop to realize the grace of this sacrament for you. In the vision, picture someone drowning in their sins, and you may evangelize that person by bringing them to Me. When the priest baptizes you, your original sin is forgiven and you are made a child of God. Again, when you fall into sin later in life, I reach out to you also in My Sacrament of Reconciliation. See how you can be saved from your sins at any time you can come to Me in confession. I wait for you to come for Me, but do not tarry. Come quickly, so I can refresh your soul and renew My life in you."*

Monday, January 13, 1997:

After Communion, I could see a hamburger in wrappings as an example of modernized food. Jesus said: *"My people, I am showing you how your technology has made your food artificial, and you have also eased all of your labors in the household. All you are doing for worldly gain has come with a cost of your health in your food and undo stress on yourselves with your fast paced jobs. You strive to get more leisure time, but you are forgetting to give Me time. Instead, many are only concerned with being entertained in some way. It is time to stop at My adoration chapels and examine what you are doing to yourselves. Take time to rest in My Spirit and value what is most important in your life. You are not here to be entertained or only to go through life's motions, but you are meant to know, love and serve Me. Following My Will for you is your goal and do not let the worldly agendas steal you away from Me. It is the heavenly things you must treasure, not the passing things of earth."*

Later, I could see some magpies making a lot of noise. I then saw a small monstrance with a Host in a recessed cove in an old Church. Jesus said: *"My people, do not be so concerned with finding out the latest news or the most recent gossip in your neighborhood. Many things change in your world, but still there is nothing truly new under the sun. Be more concerned with spending more time with Me in adoration. My love and My gift of salvation I offer to you, and I ask only for you to accept Me as ruler over your will. This is the price of your eternal salvation, that you will follow Me throughout your whole life. Give yourself as a gift to Me, and My gift to you will be eternal life with Me in heaven. When you see the real goal of your presence on earth, that is why these earthly cravings for news is so fleeting. Tomorrow's news will be sought, but today's news is quickly forgotten. Learn a lesson in treasuring what lasts forever, instead of desiring that which lasts but a moment."*

Tuesday, January 14, 1997:

After Communion, I could see a tree ablaze in fire in a park. Next to it, I could see a large waterfall. Jesus said: *"My people, as you talk about the new year, I am showing you more of your coming trials. Again, there will be continuing fires in the western part of your country whipped by strong winds. You are seeing a large waterfall, since many of your streams and rivers will be overflowing their banks. This is a continuing chastisement for all of your sins that are overflowing the cup of My justice. I love you, My people, but My purification must come to cleanse the earth of the evil that has infested it. It is very close for the harvest of souls. Take heed that you follow My directions in preparing for this culmination of evil. You will be severely tested, so strengthen your spiritual protection while you have time."*

Later, at the Maryknoll Seminary, Ossining, N.Y., before the Blessed Sacrament, I could see a soldier standing at attention with his rifle on his shoulder. Jesus said: *"My people, all of those who have been confirmed are 'Soldiers of Christ' by the power of the Holy Spirit. What you are witnessing tonight in these programs is a battle between good and evil. This is beyond a battle even, because your struggle is to save as many souls as possible through evangelization. In order to be prepared for this work, you must seek Me and ask for My graces to witness to My Word. Then when you are armed with the breastplate of faith and the sword of My justice, you will have the strength to go out and challenge the demons and evil men. Take courage, My friends, and see that your time to save souls is short. Be ever focused on Me and bring Me to these souls who are still confused by the darkness of their unbelief and the lack of trust in Me. I am the one giving the direction for your life. Listen to Me and your place in heaven will be assured."*

Wednesday, January 15, 1997:
At the Maryknoll Seminary, Ossining, N.Y., after Communion, I could see a chapel and then I was slowly walking up a small stairway in front of the Blessed Sacrament. Jesus said: *"My people, I am calling you to walk in My footsteps to your own Calvary. I came into this world to suffer and die for your sins. All those, who believe in Me, must suffer as well for My Name's sake. Some may face martyrdom, while others may have to suffer in other ways every day. I am asking you to look at your whole life as a walk to Calvary, where you must pick up your Cross and carry it for me each day. This suffering, you will experience, is a means to cleanse yourselves of your sins. By your acts of mortification and a committing of yourself to My Will, you are giving example to others and fulfilling your duty on earth that I am leading you to. Be gracious in giving of yourself and you too, will be drawn up to Me in the resurrection, that I have promised to those who accept Me as Savior. I love you so much, My people, and I desire all of My children to follow Me on the road to Calvary."*

Thursday, January 16, 1997: (Very windy day)
After Communion, I could see a marshall's badge. Jesus said: *"My people, I am showing you this badge as a symbol of the*

future police state that your country will be witnessing. Many problems with weather and famine conditions will cause food shortages as I have warned you about. Some of these shortages are planned, but the situation will deteriorate rapidly as people will be searching to find food. This chaos will go beyond the one world's plan to stage emergency powers. It is at this time that the Antichrist will take over as a man of peace to save the world. Those defying this takeover will be placed in detention centers. Pray to Me, My people, for My protection in these perilous days."

Later, at the prayer group, I could see a watchdog next to an abortion clinic. Jesus said: *"My people, I ask you to be vigilant in calling attention to your abortion mills, but not violent. Those, who truly are protecting life, would not be endangering life in using bombs. It is a strong possibility that these bombers have a different agenda in causing laws to be set up against all protesters. Pray to stop abortions as well as stopping any other violence on men."* I could see some telephone poles with phone lines going to the homes. Jesus said: *"My people, by your own news you are seeing that your privacy in conversation is easily violated. As evil men exploit various electrical devices, no one will be safe from wire-tapping or the power of suggestion on your TV. It would behoove you to rid yourself of such communications as the time of the purification comes upon you."* I could see some houses and the windows were wide open with no curtains or blinds. Jesus said. *"My people, many of you are being watched and it is almost impossible to protect yourself from the eyes of those planning the time of the Antichrist. Groundwork for your persecution is being laid down even now. Those who witness to My Name will come under strong attacks for their beliefs. Your life will be at risk to practice your faith, but your spiritual life is more precious and worth fighting to save."* I could see a crowd gathering to hear the President's Inaugural Address. Jesus said: *"My people, your president's words are eloquent, but they are like the scribes and pharisees of My day. Do as he says, but not as he does. His actions are far from Me, especially in supporting life. The eyes are a window to the soul and many times betray those who are lying. Pray for your country, that its leaders follow My ways. If you continue down the road to power and greed, many will fall by the wayside as their souls will be lost."* I could see Mary come as many people were being drawn to her places of apparition. Mary said: *"My dear children, many signs are being given to those who visit my shrines. Do not come looking for signs, but search your hearts, so you may offer my Son all of your troubles. He stands, waiting for you patiently, for your love. He seeks your love every day. If you receive some blessings, give praise and glory to God for your gifts."* I could see an amusement park with many wires all around it. Jesus said: *"My people, why are your eyes so blind to all the events that are going on around you? Many of your rights are being violated and taken away, yet many are content with watching their TV programs, and will not lift a finger to help their neighbor. You will reap the harvest of your evil age without even realizing the sins you are being chastised for."* I could see some children's toys and they were many in number. Jesus said: *"My people, many of your material things can be considered as a child would treat its toys. There is an avid enthusiasm for something new to be acquired. You will see that it is more the anticipation of getting something that holds your attention, than once you have it. Once something is possessed for a while, it soon becomes less desirable. Your spiritual life is drawing you to something permanent, instead of that which passes away with time. You will see My love draws you to an everlasting love relationship, not just a passing fancy. This is why I give you many examples, to show you that seeking things that are everlasting, should be most important in your life. Walk with Me daily and you will be with Me in heaven."*

Friday, January 17, 1997:

After Communion, I could see a bishop and then a man approach the pulpit to read or preach. Jesus said: *"My people, do not watch people to make criticism of their speech or their actions. Only your Father in heaven is liable to pass judgment on everyone. You can advise your brother of serious spiritual sins, but if he persists, only refer it to your priest. If you are judgmental in a wrongful way, consider if others treated you in the same way. In a word you must be humble and more concerned with correcting your own faults, than those of your neighbor. Also, instead of being critical, you should seize the opportunity to help your neighbor in need. In helping that person, you are helping Me as well. Look to have good intentions in your heart, and not evil designs to glorify yourself."*

Later, I saw a number of gravestones in a cemetery. Jesus said: *"My people, many will soon be tested in either witnessing to My Word, or leading souls away from the Antichrist. The faithful will be on their knees giving Me glory and their full trust. My children, the time is coming soon when all will be shown My triumph over Satan. You will see everything in Scripture being brought about. You are all being drawn to the Divine, for I desire My purification to rid the earth of all evil. See, the love I have for all of My people will be demonstrated in My coming warning. Be on guard, for My judgment can test you at any time. Be prepared for My Coming, since I will have a saving grace for all who accept Me properly into your hearts."*

Saturday, January 18, 1997:

After Communion, I could see a podium in a snowstorm. Jesus said: *"My son, you are being called to serve Me in many ways to spread my message. You must be strong and enduring in bringing a word of hope to those who need some spiritual stamina. My remnant must be prepared now for the persecution they are to undergo. Tell them that I am their only means to protect their souls, and they must seek My help to make it through this evil age. You will be tried by the elements and other forces that will try to repel you from your mission. Give up your comfort to carry out your mission as my messenger for these times."*

Later, after Communion, I was at the bottom of a tall glass building looking up as it reached into the sky. Jesus said: *"My son, as you look at the task I am asking of you, it may appear immense as this tall building. Remember, I am not asking you to go out alone. I will give you strength through my blessings, and I have told you to seek the power of the Holy Spirit in your speech. The readings are talking of My messengers and they are witnessing to how I call all of you to be My disciples in preaching the Gospel. When you are travelling, remember also, to witness your struggle against the abortions in your country. Draw the connec-*

tion of these weather chastisements to the abortions in your country. Pray that more women will change their hearts and carry their babies to full term. I love and cherish My servants as I encourage you in your ministry."

At Nocturnal Hour, I saw a man holding a bundle of wheat heads and there were several beds with sick people. Jesus said: *"My people, I am showing you this vision, since you will be tested by famine and plagues. Strange sicknesses will afflict the people and they will have many sores all over their bodies. Food will be in short supply, and eventually, it will be controlled by the one world people. You will be visited by various plagues of disease and pests until many will die or wish they were dead. All of these trials will be brought to show you how dependent on Me you need to be. You will be stripped of your comforts when the electricity and gas are no longer available. Pray for My help and I will guide you through even the worst of trials."*

Sunday, January 19, 1997:

I could see an African tribesman with a spear and a large shield. Jesus said: *"My son, you are seeing the shield I am setting up at the proper time to protect you from the attacks of the evil one. Your time right now is very precious, which is why I am making these many opportunities available to you. Take advantage of this time and preach My message of love and forgiveness, while you still can. Help Me in saving souls and your reward will be given you. If you become lazy, you will be chastised into doing My work, despite your resistance. Do not worry about time or what people think, and proceed on your path to evangelize as many souls as you can. Your preparation is needed now to wake up the people."*

Monday, January 20, 1997:

I could see a fold-up chair standing and then someone unfolded it and sat down on it. Jesus said: *"My people, you need to make some time for Me out of your busy schedules. If you cannot sit down with your Lord for a short time, then you are doing too much. Come to Me in adoration before My Blessed Sacrament, and I will give you my gifts of peace and rest in My spirit. Those, who truly love Me, are willing to answer this request.*

*While you are before Me, I can communicate My love to you.
Also, say a prayer there for all those who do not take the time to
come and see Me. Pray for all sinners that they may wake up
soon and rejoice in My forgiveness, before they may lose their
souls to the evil one."*

Later, I could see some large state rooms in a big building.
There was a large dinner table and many men were all seated around
it. Jesus said: *"My people, the one world government is controlling the events as they happen. They dictate things of money and
jobs. They will be controlling money, food, and communications.
All of these tools are being put in place to aid the Antichrist's
coming. These plans have been made for many years in advance
of this time. So when you see the helicopters, the UN troops, and
the mark of the beast come at the beginning of the tribulation,
these will be signs to you of the height of evil. My moment of
victory is not far away. My Second Coming is but a short time
from now. Take heed of My Words of love and place your hope
and trust in Me. With Me at your right side, your soul will have
its protection."*

Tuesday, January 21, 1997:

After Communion, I could see a poor person and there were
boxes all around them. Jesus said: *"My people, each of you have
your own sphere of influence and the duties in life you attend to
each day. You see these boxes as the range of your activities. I am
asking you, My friends, to go beyond your cares and look for
opportunities to help those less fortunate than yourselves. Give a
helping hand to the poor, since many will forget them and walk
by. Make their needs one of your responsibilities, so you can go
out of your comfort zone to help your neighbor. In reaching out
to My little ones, you are reaching out to Me in My need. Share
the many gifts that I have given you, so you are not selfish with
your abundance."*

Later, I could see a strong vision of plants blooming as in the
Era of Peace. Then, I saw a night scene where people were walking through flames of fire. Jesus said: *"Yes, My son, you are being
attacked this night, since the evil one does not want people to be
saved through these messages. You are seeing the beauty of My*

vegetation in the era of peace. My glory will put forth the shoots of glorious plants all over the earth. Men, who live during this time, will be thankful to see this day. The second vision is about the three days of darkness, when the evil men will be chastised by fire in the justice of My purification. All of those, who rejected Me and chose the Antichrist instead, will have to pay for their crimes and suffer the flames of hell forever. The evil one does not want people to know they are responsible for their sins. When My light shines on the darkness, it exposes evil for what it is — a defiance of My love and My truth. Listen to Me O people of the earth. Now is the time when you will be forced to decide between Me and Satan. You will choose between a glorious day with Me in heaven or a horrific eternity in the flames of hell — suffering the insults and taunts from the abuse of the demons."

Wednesday, January 22, 1997:

After Communion, it was dark and I saw a light shining on the floor where a podium stood in the rain. Jesus said: *"My son, you are My messenger to go out and dispel the darkness of sin, where people are not obeying My commands. Sin is being forgotten as well as the responsibility for one's actions. Even though it is unpopular and the rain indicates rejection, you must go and preach conversion and repenting of their sins to all. Give witness to My love, My mercy, and My justice. Show the people that unless they repent of their sins, they cannot enter into My Kingdom. This is man's problem throughout the centuries, that he must give his will over to me and seek my pardon of his sins. Without being sorry for your sins, you will remain in darkness and My light will not enter your soul."*

Thursday, January 23, 1997:

After Communion, I could see Maria E. and she was praying. Then I saw a cameraman taking pictures of the protest of abortions. Jesus said: *"My people, you are witnessing this march against abortion in your country. It is almost as a funeral march for all the babies killed in your land. Yet, still many women are not listening, and they would rather kill their babies out of convenience or for money. Who can place a value on a life that I have created? When you put a price on life, you cheapen it, and give license to kill at your own whim. You are not God, since you do not have the power to give and take life. I tell you, if abortions are not stopped in your country, there will be another funeral. Only this time, it will by your own, for your country will be destroyed and taken over. If you flaunt the gifts of life that I give you, I will remove the blessings I have favored your country with in the past. My justice must reign where sin abounds. Your killing causes Me to suffer still more on the cross for your sins of abortion."*

At the prayer group, I could see a small parish church and then a large dark figure approached the church to close it. Jesus said: *"My people, you are seeing a gradual takeover by evil forces as the time of the tribulation approaches. Gradually, your churches will be closed one by one as the number of priests declines and government harassment continues. As you will have trouble finding Mass, an underground church will be forming to protect the heritage of your faith. You have My mother's rosary to carry you on in the absence of the Mass. Pray much for My protection in this time."* I could see a bright light as a guardian angel was watching over a young child. Jesus said: *"My people, My angels are always watching over My little ones. They report any injustices as they happen. I am especially saddened when these angels come to Me as an abortion occurs. I give My angels a special mission to watch over every one of My children. These heavenly beings are constantly advising you just as the demons are tempting you to do evil. Listen to the advice of your angels and follow your inclinations to do good. I see everything you do. Nothing escapes My eye. Be ever on the watch to follow My Word and reject the desires of the world."* I could see a woman with a closet full of new dresses and she was standing in front of a mirror. Jesus said: *"Be careful, My people, that you do not get too taken up with your outward appearance. Be prudent in your appearance, but not excessive. Instead of looking in the mirror to better your physical appearance, look into your soul and see if you are following My commands and acts of mercy. If you treated your soul's appearance before Me as you take care of your dress before men, many would be a lot holier. Seek a bal-*

ance in your spiritual life and do things to please Me instead of pleasing yourself." I could see a dove come representing the Holy Spirit. The Holy Spirit said: *"I am the Spirit of Love and I come as the flame indicated tonight to bless all those here with the flame of My love. I bless you and strengthen you to go out and fight this battle to preserve life, especially your fight against abortions. Do not hesitate to witness your displeasure with your country's bad ruling on abortion. Pray and act to do what you can to stop abortions. I will guide those who are active in this fight."* I saw Mary holding her suffering Son. Mary said: *"My dear children, why to do continue to cause My son to suffer? Every time you sin, he must make up in suffering for that offense. As your sins are more serious, He must suffer even more. When you see statues weeping tears or blood, you are seeing the effects of sin. All sin needs recompense. This is why many suffering servants are making atonement for the sins of man. You can diminish this suffering by restraining your sins. For every sin you do not commit, this is one less suffering that will be needed. You can help also by praying for sinners and atone in your prayers to keep this balance of good with evil."* I could see a beautiful altar in a chapel where the Blessed Sacrament was exposed for Adoration. Jesus said: *"Come, My children, and visit Me often. I am a prisoner in the Host, but I have chosen this so to make Myself available to those who would want to come to Me. This Presence is a pouring out of My love for all of mankind. Take advantage of this opportunity to be with Me while you still can. Give Me your troubles and I will give you My rest. Give Me your petitions and I will answer your prayers according to My Will. You will treasure your visits as you will glow with My love."* I could see a bright white full moon in the night (as tonight in actuality). Jesus said: *"My people, as you look at this pure white disk, think of it as your soul after a good confession. Many clouds and phases of time tend to darken this light. This is the way your sins draw Me away from you and this is how serious sin blots out your soul's life in darkness. Come to My light by seeking forgiveness of your sins in confession. Continue this renewal of grace to keep your souls as beacons of light to all around you."*

Friday, January 24, 1997:

After Communion, I could see a dam as it was overflowing and there was a great rainstorm. God the Father came and He said: *"I Am is coming to judge America. How long will you continue to offend Me with your many sins? Your sins are overflowing My cup of justice as you see this water overflowing this dam. Through all the messages given you, you still will not repent. How long do you expect Me to hold back my hand? You have seen the great flood and the fire of Sodom and Gomorrah. Are you any less guilty with all of your killings? I tell you, that you will be and are being chastised for your sins. These storms will be relentless, until you wake up and come to your knees in honoring Me and My Commandments. I have a great love for man, but man must acknowledge his Creator. Come to Me out of love or come to Me out of fear, but come."*

Later, I could see St. Therese coming and she said: *"My son, you must be careful in taking pride in your work. Do everything for the glory of God, not just to impress your peers or let curiosity lead you away from your thoughts on God. Do not forget to allow Jesus some time for prayer, even in your busy schedule. If it be necessary, refuse other activities, so you can allot your prayer time. In your mission, you must protect your prayer life and keep a proper focus on Jesus at all times, even in the workplace. For those successes you are blessed with, give thanks to God and give Him the glory. In all of your behavior, keep a humble attitude, so people will not praise you, but only God. You are a recipient of many gifts. Use them properly for the Lord and He will give you a reward for knowing your place. Offer all of your actions each day to Jesus, so your work will become a prayer and not something to seek praise from men."*

Saturday, January 25, 1997:

After Communion, I could see a bishop talking with some people. Jesus said: *"My people, pray for My shepherds to protect them from the attacks of the evil one. My bishops have a great responsibility to many of My faithful. They need to give good example in their teaching and protect themselves with a good prayer life. Some of My bishops have been misled and they fol-*

low their own agendas instead of Mine. This is why you must pray to help those wayward bishops even more and support them in a friendly manner. By your good example to them, you may encourage them to change their ways. Part of their responsibility is to encourage those men who want to be priests. Pray again that your church leaders will teach the new priests the proper traditions, and not worldly pursuits only."

Later, I could see a seat belt restraining me around my waist. Jesus said: *"My son, you have been allowed to publish the messages and go freely to preach My message. There is coming an increase in evil where people will have more difficulties in allowing you to speak. These difficulties will increase as the souls being touched increases. Satan will be closing ears and hearts to your message as ridicule will increase. Many, who accepted your messages at first, will find it increasingly hard to believe, when their lifestyles are compromised. Gradually, your speaking will diminish as hearts will grow cold to Me and men will listen to the Antichrist and his agents. Do not let criticism and few numbers discourage you. If one soul is saved in one of your trips, it has been a success. Know, My son, that these and more difficulties will come your way, as men will persecute you for your beliefs. I am with you to the end, so never stop witnessing until your body can no longer move. It is important for souls that you carry on this struggle against evil. Pray much, and go where I send you to preach the Good News of salvation. Thank you for all you are doing, for your reward will be great."*

Sunday, January 26, 1997:

After Communion, I could see a sword. This is the same sword we pierce Jesus' heart when we sin. Jesus said: *"My people, you are seeing the pain your sins are causing Me. Instead of showing Me your love, your sins are as swords thrust into My heart in defiance of My love. The readings speak of a call to conversion. I have come to earth to die on the Cross for your sins. I am offering each person salvation and I am suffering to atone for your sins against the Father, but I give each of you a free will to come to Me out of love and seek forgiveness of your sins. You must be sorry for your sins and willing to come forth publicly in confession to have them forgiven. Your mortal or serious sins must be confessed to a priest before receiving Me in Holy Communion. It is this public witness you must acknowledge before men, before I will publicly witness you to My Father in heaven. By your contrition for sin you need to continually be renewed through confession to keep your soul beautiful in grace before Me. I instituted this Sacrament of Penance or Reconciliation as a means to conversion for even the hardest of sinners to return to Me. Seek My love and forgiveness constantly, and you will be perfecting yourself to lessen the sins that most offend Me. Come into My loving arms, and receive My love and graces that will keep you close to Me."*

Later, I could see a house with a tall fence all around it. Then I was traveling down a road in the winter time, and I could see some electrical lines. Jesus said: *"My people, you have been gifted with much information about the times which are near. Look around you, and see the signs of the one world government about to take control. Little by little they will be controlling your food, your power, your fuel, your money, and your communications. All of this has been planned for years, as preparations are being made for the Antichrist to assume power. I have told you many times to be prepared to go into hiding. Remember you are in a battle with evil spirits and evil men. You are to prepare most with your spiritual weapons. Do not be so concerned with the body, but fight to preserve your souls. Call on My angels to fight your battles. This evil is strong, but it can be overcome with love, prayers and the power I will give your guardian angels. Pray for My guidance in this time and alert the people for all of these battles that will come to a head shortly. With full trust in Me, I will protect you and lead you to safe places. Be ready, My children, for your time of freedom is running out."*

Monday, January 27, 1997:
After Communion, I could see a sarcophagus of a small infant which represented an Egyptian tomb, as an epitaph of our country's place in history. Jesus said: *"My people, your American society will show history that your country decayed by killing its own infants. Your moral decay was followed by drugs and*

*the destruction of the family. It was your worship of material-
ism, instead of God, that has sealed your fate. Without immi-
grants, your numbers would be decreasing. Even amidst such
sin, you still do not realize your imminent ruin from the forces
of your evil age. As the height of evil draws to its conclusion,
you will see that your last state will be worse that your first.
Prepare, My friends, to meet the fate of your punishment, as My
purification will cleanse the earth of all evil. Those, who search
for justice, will soon have their day."*

Later, I could see some huge doors to the temple open as a
symbol of the First Covenant in the Old Testament. Jesus said:
*"My people, a covenant was made with the Hebrews through
Moses to follow the Ten Commandments in exchange that God
would have them as his chosen people. Another covenant was
made even from the time Adam and Eve left the Garden of Eden,
that God would send a redeemer to save all of mankind. I have
come and fulfilled all the prophecies about Me, but My suffering
for man's sins is still going on. I have promised to be faithful to
men in offering salvation to every soul that seeks Me. You, for
your part, must fulfill the other part of My Covenant and come to
Me in acceptance of My being your Savior. This requires that
you be converted from your sins and that you seek My forgiveness. Remember, there are two parties to each covenant and each
party must meet their end of the agreement. I love all of you with
an infinite and perfect love, but you must love Me in return. By
treasuring this love through frequent confession, you can keep
this love covenant alive and burning in your heart. Remember
My love constantly, until the day you die."*

Tuesday, January 28, 1997: (St. Thomas Aquinas)
After Communion, I could see four people above me looking
down on me. Jesus said: *"My son, you will see many read your
books and My messages. Some will read them with a critical eye
trying to discredit them. Others will find the messages too fright-
ening to accept, or too hard for them to change their lives. Still
others, with an open heart will accept them, and many will be
converted, as I have told you before. I tell you, when they are
examined, they will be found to have My love deeply touching*

the lives of My people. I have brought forth these teachings and warnings, so the faith may be upheld and the people may prepare their hearts and souls for My Second Coming. Now is the acceptable time to be saved. My arms are always open to receive anyone willing to accept Me. Come to Me now before it is too late, and you will be lost to Satan. Seek my love, and not the evil one's lies and hate."

Later, I could see a stage with Lenin's picture at the Russian Parliament. Jesus said: *"My people, you are seeing this picture in Russia, since there is a power struggle going on for its leadership. If some belligerent leader should take over, it could mean a possible nuclear threat either to the U.S. or China. Keep your eye on this leadership situation, since this is a power that the Antichrist could tap into. Pray for peace in the world, since man is always trying to gain more than he needs. Many conflicts are fought for power and greed for land and riches. Pray for your leaders that they may come to their senses, instead of starting World War III. A major war is possible. Only prayer and people's sharing in love can stop war. War is brought on through hate and the sins of man. Always seek love and good to battle the hate and evil from the dark side."*

Wednesday, January 29, 1997:

After Communion, I could see a fire in a hearth and then it went out. Jesus said: *"My people, when you see a fire for heating, you know it requires some care for fuel and air flow. It is the same way with the flames of love. To love someone, you have to know and understand about that person's existence. This is why if you are to love Me, you must study the Scriptures to know My Will for you. The fuel for your love for Me is an understanding of Me, and all the gifts that I give you. Your response to keeping this love alive is the gifts that you give back to Me. The air or oxygen to keep that fire of love burning, is the perseverance you show in loving Me. I wait for you always with an unconditional love. You must think every day to remember Me in your prayers, and follow My Will. The harvest of love is when you can spread My love to others. This is how you can have 30, 60, and 100 fold return on My love."*

Thursday, January 30, 1997:

After Communion, I could see a flame on a candle lying horizontally and in the background there was a cave. This was indicating the time of the three days of darkness, where I saw a massive cleansing fire. Jesus said: *"My son, I am showing you another vision of what it will be like during the three days of darkness. You are seeing a flame burn on a horizontal position to show you My miraculous help in protecting My faithful from harm. Only blessed candles will give you light from matches. I have told you not to look at My wrath of justice on the condemned. Those, who look, will be punished in My own way. The flame, you see, will be a purifying fire, that will cleanse the earth of all evil. It is a sign also that all evil men and the demons will be cast into hell at that time. This is the moment of My triumph as some of My faithful will be safe in the caves I will provide."*

At the prayer group, I could see a boy of about one year old. Jesus said: *"My people, you parents have the spiritual responsibility to bring up your children in the faith. See that they are baptized and taken to weekly Mass, so they can see the importance of God, in both your life and their lives. As they grow up, see to it that they are taught the faith at home and school. They should be educated in the faith, as well as they are educated in secular things. Teach them their prayers and give them good example in your actions."* I could see the faces of several people who had just died, but I did not know them. Jesus said: *"My people, many times I have asked you to be on guard to protect your souls by keeping them cleansed frequently with confession. Then should it be your turn to die, you will be ready to come to Me. Your spiritual welfare is not anything you can put off, since you never know when it is your turn to die. As people die around you, let this be a gentle reminder that when you come before Me, all accounts must be settled at your judgment. Keep a strong love for Me, so I can claim you are mine, instead of the devil's victim."* I could see some filing cabinets where records were stored. Jesus said: *"My people, during your lives, you can commit many sins, some of which you have never confessed. If you come to Me in confession and reveal your sins to the priest, they will be forgiven, and those also that you innocently have forgotten. If you do not come*

to My Sacrament of Reconciliation, your sins cannot be forgiven. It is your admitting your sins, and your contrition for them, that I wipe them out of My memory. Woe to those who do not confess their sins, since they will be held accountable. My mercy is poured out over sinners, but you must seek My forgiveness, if you wish to have eternal life." I could see a large pipe pouring out pollution into a stream. Jesus said: "*My people, look to your words and actions, that you are not pouring out a pollution of evil that may influence those around you. Parents and adults should be role models of good living, especially to younger people. Watch your anger and your tongue that you do not swear or are critical of others. If you are beacons of love, you will have a good influence and contribute to peace in the world. If you show hate or sin in your actions, you are adding to evil and causing unrest which could lead to wars. Know how much you influence others by your presence. See to it that you carry out My Will.*" I could see some government monuments to some past presidents. Jesus said: "*My people, history is the best judge of how your laws and decrees have guided your civilization. Empires rise and they fall. The degree, that you keep My Commandments in your laws, will determine how long your governing will last. As you see your laws and decisions become more corrupt, you are challenging My justice. Those, who refuse Me, I will withdraw My blessings and you will quickly fall in a heap of ruble. See your faults and reform your ways or you will be destroyed as empires before you.*"
I could see Mary come to some children. Mary said: "*My dear children, listen to the words of my messengers and take my words to heart. Read them over, if you have forgotten them, but do not forget them. I give you words of wisdom to live by, especially for these times. Many of my messengers are no longer receiving messages. This is another sign to you that my Son's Second Coming is not far off.*" I could see a train that was carrying some strange marked heavy boxes. Jesus said: "*Be on guard, My people, for many guns and troops are being moved around in your country, many of which are part of the UN. The one world people are readying their plans for a world coup to make way for the Antichrist. Do not be surprised how vulnerable your people will be to these evil forces. Ready your forces for good in spiritual prepara-*

tion for the tribulation. Fighting is not what I desire, but rely on Me, and your angels to fight your battles."

Friday, January 31, 1997:

After Communion, I could see a poor lady with children waiting at a bus station. Jesus said: *"My people, there are some of you who do not have opportunities to make a good wage. As a result, many, who have the same needs to survive, are left in want of even essentials to living. Think of how you would have to live on a meager salary. Pray for the poor among you that they do not lose heart. People without the basics either are not taught about Me, or find it difficult to get to Church. Help the poor in any way that you can, and do not deprive them of food and education. Think of what they have to deal with, and your heart will go out to them."*

Later, at Barry's Bay, Ontario, Canada, in Adoration, at Bob and Rita McDonald's home, I could see a bishop with red flowers by him. Jesus said: *"My people, My bishops and cardinals are in revolt. They honor the Holy Father with their lips, but their hearts are far from Me. Some of My own leaders are harboring thoughts of how to exile My pope son, and install one of their own leaders. This newly elected pope will give them what they want, but it will come at the cost of a schism in My Church. This new pope will have evil roots and will mislead many away from Me, as he will declare many heresies valid. Do not be deceived by this imposter pope, who will be very subtle at first, but gradually will even accept the leadership of the Antichrist. This first beast comes with lies and deceits that will even persuade some of My elect. Refuse all of his teachings and hold fast to the teachings I have given My apostles. I will watch over you, if you seek Me to help you in this tribulation."*

Saturday, February 1, 1997:

At St. Hedwig's Church, Barry's Bay, Ontario, Canada, after Communion, I could see a vision of Pope John Paul II with a light shining about him. Jesus said: *"My people, I have sent you My pope son as a special grace, especially for this time. I ask you to follow him and listen to all of his decrees and writings. He is the one to teach you faith and morals as given from My apostles. This is the line of succession of St. Peter that I have promised to protect My Church. There are some who refuse to accept My pope son's teachings, and also his authority. He is a vicar of My Church, and suffers much from those who do not believe faithfully to My traditions. Even though there is dissention abound, still I give all of you strength through My sacraments to uphold the eternal truths proclaimed in My revelation. Rejoice, My children, for My Word is truth, for all who would believe. Those, wishing to follow their own will, will have to be judged according to their own deeds. Pray to be holy and I will protect your faith in Me from the evil one."*

Later, at St. Hedwig's Church, Barry's Bay, Ontario, Canada, after Communion, I could see people entering a narrow hallway. Then I could see a glorious banquet with people walking in white robes. Jesus said: *"My people, enter through the narrow gate to heaven, and avoid the broad road to hell. For a while you must suffer trials and tribulations, but this will soon come to pass. You must follow My Will, if you are to gain eternal life with Me in heaven. I come for each of you as a hound of heaven seeking your soul's love until you die. See how My love embraces you from your conception. For those, who accept Me and follow Me, I will open the gates to the glory of My Kingdom. In the vision you are seeing those with their washed robes entering into the peace and love of being with Me for eternity. Seek your soul's desire by following My Commandments, and asking My forgiveness of your sins. Your life's desire will be fulfilled in Me more than you could ever imagine. I love you and I ask you to come to Me always every day."*

Sunday, February 2, 1997: (Feast of St. Blaise, Presentation in the Temple)

At Barry's Bay, at Adoration in Rita and Bob McDonald's home, Ontario, Canada, I could see an arrow being held by an eagle. On the other side the eagle held an olive branch of peace. Jesus said: *"My people, you will see many threats to your freedom come and you will have two choices. Some patriots will chose to take up arms against the one world agents, but I tell My faithful, to seek into the bush for hiding. I do not want you to take up arms in fighting. Satan for many years has tricked you into fighting wars. This was because he hates man and wants all of you dead. So, if you do not kill, you are frustrating his attempts to have you fighting. This is a hard lesson, not to fight for your freedom, but you must submit to My Will in this request. Even if you are to be martyred, do not fight your persecutors. As I suffered, you too must suffer for a while. Your reward will be to live with Me in the new era of peace, for those who remain faithful. You must have love and peace according to My will, if you are to witness to My love. Show love to all, even to your enemies who wish to kill you. This is a perfect love I ask, because it is a selfless love. Your love for Me must be constantly seeking perfection in preparation for your being with Me eternally in heaven."*

Later, at St. Hedwig's Church, Barry's Bay, Ontario, Canada, after Communion, I could see the top roof of a temple from the inside, and Jesus was being presented. Then I could see a land of snow with a purifying white color. Jesus said: *"My children, you are first presented to Me in Baptism, where your original sin is purified, and you are welcomed into My Church. This pure soul is carried on and continually purified through the grace of My Sacrament of Reconciliation. Now, as you draw close to the end times, you will see another purification. When you see the white snow, it is nature's way to cleanse the landscape and give it a beauty for you to see. So it is when I will cleanse the world of evil. All will be made beautiful once again. Prepare now to meet your Lord, when I come triumphant on the clouds of My glory. Remain faithful in prayer and you will be brought forth into the peace and love of My era of peace."*

Monday, February 3, 1997:

After Communion, I could see a cave as a place for hiding from persecution. Jesus said: *"My people, just as in days gone by, men used caves as protection from evil men persecuting them for their religious beliefs. Many will not accept the Christians of your day either. You may find yourselves seeking such shelter as well. With My angels I will provide for your protection. You may suffer giving up your comforts, but you will want to protect your souls more. Learn your priorities in life, that My protection for your soul is most important. You will be thankful for My help right before I call the evil men and spirits to their judgment. Rejoice, My people, the end of this evil age is in sight. I will test you for a time, but then I will reward My remnant faithful in ways they could not dream of."*

Later, Adoration I could see a picture of the Capitol, and then some black helicopters came swooping right toward me. I then saw someone having the chip placed in their right hand and a little blood came forth. The helicopters were controlling the crowds to get their mark of the beast. Jesus said: *"My people, the time of your trial is about to begin. I have shown you in every way possible how the technology and the people are in position to implement the mark of the beast. You will see events move quickly, since Satan has only a short time left. The chips, as you have told the people, are in fact ready to be deployed. The one world people will subtly bring the chip to the public, encouraging them of its advantages. Then, they will try to force you to take the chip. This is where the detention centers and the helicopters will be used for crowd control, for the dissenters who do not want to take the chip. Soon you will have to go into hiding as I have told you. All of the messages are coming to an open understanding of these events. Remember never to take the chip in your hand or forehead or you will be lost. Those, who think they can remove it, will be deceived, since the Antichrist will then control you. As soon as the chips have been placed in the people, the Antichrist will take control over all of the nations. See, My children, that these events are imminent and prepare spiritually and physically to fight the evil forces. Keep your trust and hope in Me that I will protect you. I will shorten this trial, and soon declare My triumph as I purify the earth. Have patience but a moment and I will bring you to the glory of My Kingdom."*

Tuesday, February 4, 1997:

After Communion, I could see a beam from outer space coming down toward me. Jesus said: *"My son, you will come under increasing attack from powers who want to prevent your evangelization of the people. You will see delays and other means to thwart you from your mission. Pray much for angelic help and be quick in avoiding problems. Satan will be growing in power and influence for a time. See these attempts to stop you as a spiritual battle which you will be facing more and more. Be prepared to go that extra mile for Me, no matter how many inconveniences you may encounter. You are seeing a massive battle between good and evil going on at this time. Seek My help every day to fight this battle. Seek your guardian angel in this work as well. My love is with you, and My strength to endure your trial will always be available to you."*

Wednesday, February 5, 1997:
    After Communion, I could see a loving and compassionate face of Jesus up close. Jesus said: *"My people, My love is poured out on all of My faithful. Those, who have the gift of faith, have a rich treasure indeed. The people of My town questioned My authority, since they thought they knew of My origins. Even today, it is hard for men to understand that I died for their sins. I am their Savior and their way to heaven. Many times it is the eyes seen through the world's standard, that blinds men from understanding Me through the eyes of faith. Therefore, you should live by My laws and My example, instead of your own. Many of My messengers have had the same problems in their towns, but listen to the message of love I send to your hearts. See that it is the spiritual life which is most important. When you nourish the spirit with My sacraments, this is the best way to draw yourself close to Me. Believe, and have faith in My words and your spiritual destination with Me will be assured."*
    Later, I could see police at night trying to stop some riots over food shortages. Jesus said: *"My people, this is a serious message, because it is a foretaste of the turmoil that will be going on in your country. I have told you of the famine coming, and for everyone to set aside some food. Some have listened, but most have either not heard this message, or they have refused to believe it. The one world people will use this chastisement to control the people through their food. There will be a tremendous chaos as people will clear out the stores of food, and riots will develop when hungry people search for food. Your low food supplies will*

be controlled and sold eventually only to those with the mark of the beast. As this turmoil comes, you will need to flee with your angels into hiding places. Those, seeking food and stability, will easily welcome the Antichrist who will offer to settle the strife going on with his peace. Many will be taken in by the Antichrist's promises, but you, My friends, will have to depend on Me to feed and protect you. Even under pain of death, refuse any help or the mark of the beast from the evil ones. Pray that you will be strong and faithful in this test. I alone will lead you to victory. Fight the evil ones with only your spiritual weapons."

Thursday, February 6, 1997:

After Communion, I could see a flower garden enclosed with a white tile border. Jesus said: *"My people, as you see this indoor garden, you know it takes care to heat, water and feed the garden nutrients. In some ways this is how much I take care of all of you on earth. I hold the elements and stars in place to give you a friendly environment to live. You have means at your disposal to provide your own food through work on your part. Most of all, I add tender loving care to you by My spiritual presence in My sacraments. I am always available to you in listening to your prayers and petitions. You are better than plants, since you can love Me in return and give Me gifts as well."*

Later, at the prayer group, I could see a large black cat with its teeth showing. Jesus said: *"My people, you are seeing this cat as those evil men who would wish to consume you. Many of My children have fallen prey to the ways of the one world people. You will be tested and persecuted for your belief in My Name. Come to Me for help at this time, and I will protect you. Many seek a place to be safe, but you will only be safe in My arms when you seek Me in prayer."* I could see the mountains of Pennsylvania where we will be traveling. Jesus said: *"My son, you are giving up your weekend to evangelize and prepare My people. As you help souls, you will continually be tested in reparation for those you will be touching. See that these souls have a price that you may have to suffer for. Time is short to evangelize souls back to Me. Be in haste to help all those whom you can see. Show them the depth of My love and enrich their faith by seeking the sacraments, especially confession of their sins.*" I could see coverings over statues as the time for Lent draws near. Jesus said: *"My people, this Lent will be a special time of preparation for you. Make your plans now how you can best make some self-sacrifices for your sins. It is by self-denial that your spirit will have more control over your bodily needs. Make some time to get closer to Me this Lent. Let this be a time of meditation on My gifts and blessings, so you can give Me proper thanks. Do not just take the ashes in initial fervor, and not keep up your good intentions. Pray to stick by your offering throughout all of Lent. Let this season not pass such that you will move forward in your faith.*" I could see many people protesting in the streets. Jesus said: *"My people, there are many trouble spots in your world today. Many injustices are abound and some societies are calling their leaders to task. People can control their destiny by those they elect. Even if leaders try to force their will on the people, it may return on them. Pray for your leaders to be just in their dealings. If they abuse their powers, they will have to answer to Me and the ire of the people.*" I could see Mary come and she was holding up her mantle around Medjugorje. Mary said: *"My dear children, listen to the call for prayers from My little ones in Medjugorje. A call for prayers for peace in your world is being pursued. Protect your prayer life, and pray for a deliverance from the trials to come. I will be watching over all of My children. Continue your rosaries for My intentions.*" I could see a large cafeteria and it was empty except for a figure of death sitting at one table. Jesus said: *"My people, I have asked you to take serious, this request to prepare some food for the coming famine. You will see some even die of starvation in various places. Even more important, is the spiritual starvation that many souls have deprived themselves of in My sacraments. Come to Me often and I will care for your souls. When you visit Me in adoration, you will receive special graces to bear the difficulties of your daily life.*" I could see a gleaming gold crown in the clouds as a brilliant white light shown outward as Jesus came as King of the Universe. Jesus said: *"My people, see that My triumph is not far off. I wish you to share in the glory of My Kingship. Share in My love as I call all of you to heaven. Keep strong in your faith, so you may enjoy My reign over all peoples. This love I am willing to share even now, but when My glorious Kingdom comes, you will rejoice to see My day. This is when you will see Me all powerful and Satan tied up in chains. Your life then will be heaven on earth. Pray now, so you can prepare yourself for the coming trial. Your reward with Me will be well worth anything you must suffer for My sake."*

Friday, February 7, 1997:

After Communion, I could see about eight faces in front of me, but their identity was blotted out. Jesus said: *"My son, these are the souls in most need of your help through Me. I want you to offer up your prayers and your day's sufferings for them. Your mission is for saving souls, but you must be armed with My blessings which I will send you. To do My mission requires a strong faith, and a strong will to overcome the many obstacles in your way. Pray to the Holy Spirit for help in your work for what to say and whom to pray over. I go with you on every trip, and I am guiding all you do for My glory and praise. Be ever thankful for all the graces to be on this mission. Constantly, give Me praise and the glory for all that is happening. Time is short and you must take advantage to go while you can."*

Saturday, February 8, 1997:

At St. John Neumann's Church, Philadelphia, Pa., after Communion, I could see a bishop saying Mass at the altar. St. John Neumann gave the message: *"My son, I am happy to greet you*

today and thank you for reverencing me in your prayer group. Jesus comes to shepherd His people whenever they call on Him. The people of His day were hungry for His words of teaching, His words of love and His acts of healing. As I witnessed to the Lord's people, you also must go forward to witness Jesus' words to his flock. You have been called on a special mission at this time to call on men and women to conversion. Anytime is appropriate for conversion, but in these end times, it is an extra urgency that people prepare for the Second Coming of Jesus. Pray sincerely and humbly over God's people, that they may reverence Jesus more in his Blessed Sacrament. The Lord is especially thankful to all of His workers in spreading the Gospel message to repent."

Sunday, February 9, 1997:

At St. Mary's Church, Bedford, N.J., after Communion, I could see a Church with stained glass windows and there was a wedding service being performed. Jesus said: *"My people, I have given all of you a calling to your vocation in life, since I have a plan for each of you. I draw your attention to the Sacrament of Marriage where I have blessed man and wife to bring forth life and share in My creation of new souls. This gift of marriage is such a symbol of love, that I have used this union to show My love for you in My Church. Always remember to love one another, and My spouses. I encourage you to remain faithful to your vows of love until you die. My love for you is everlasting. Continue to be faithful to Me as well in following My Will. The vocation to the priesthood is also a blessed vocation, so I can bring My Presence to you in the sacraments. Praise Me for this gift of the priesthood for your salvation. Pray for your priests, and continue to support their ministries through all of your trials and tribulations. I love all of you in any vocation that you are called to. Join with Me in every step of your life, to walk with Me to your salvation in heaven."*

Later, at Adoration, I could see a body laid out in a casket. It was revealed to me that this was the death of our freedoms in America. Jesus said: *"My people of the United States, the bell is tolling for you. You have prided yourselves over such a government for the free, but I tell you, evil men have a plan to usurp all of your freedoms. Your country was founded on Christian prin-*

ciples, and I have blessed you with many graces. Now, your sins have caused you to turn your back on Me. All nations, who turn Me away, are ripe for destruction. You are no exception, since soon you will be taken over by foreign UN troops. Your president, through his unconstitutional use of emergency executive orders, will be in league with evil men to sell you out to the one world powers behind the UN. You will see tyrannical use of power hold your people captive, ready for the Antichrist's takeover. Through the chip in your hands, evil men will try to control you. Flee, My children, at this time into hiding, so the evil men will not control you. Never give in to taking the mark of the beast, but trust in My care only, and I will see to your needs in a miraculous way."

Monday, February 10, 1997:

After Communion, I could see some folding chairs and a party going on before Lent. Jesus said: *"My people, many of you like to indulge in your excesses before you start Lent. This points up even more the battle going on between the body and the spirit. Due to the sin of Adam, you have been weakened by sin and are vulnerable to many temptations. This is why Lent is an excellent time to mortify the body and hold it in check by self-denial. Do not see Lent as a drudgery, but a beautiful time for the spirit to grow in your faith. Concentrate on doing things to bring your soul closer to Me. Do not waste this opportunity to train yourself in better devotions, such that your life will be directed closer to follow My Will. Make your plans now how you will test the body, to be more under control by the spirit."*

Later, at Adoration, I could see a priest presenting an ornate gold box to the altar. Inside the box was represented the gift of life given to each of us. Jesus said: *"My people, as you have read of My creation today, think of how valuable life is to all of you. You are created from the dust of the earth, and I place My Spirit of life in each of you. At the end of your life, your spirit will leave your body and the body will decay back to the dust whence it came. In between the beginning and the end of life, you are here to show Me where you desire to be. Either you will love Me and follow My Will, or you will praise yourself and follow your own devices. You decide by your actions where you are destined to go. Use this Lent, My friends, to direct your lives closer to Me. Look and examine where you are on life's path. Remember, it is following My Will and seeking My forgiveness for your sins that will show your love for Me and your neighbor. Seek to carry your cross with more vigor in your Lenten devotions. Follow My steps to Calvary, since all of you must suffer life's trials and frustrations. Call on Me to help walk with you through life, and then you will see at your resurrection how I will reunite your body and your spirit. Then you will no longer be corruptible, but a child and saint of God."*

Tuesday, February 11, 1997: (Feast of Our Lady of Lourdes)
After Communion, I could see Our Lady come, followed by a vision of the grotto in Lourdes, France. Mary said: *"My dear children, I am indeed the Immaculate Conception and guardian of your country, who claims me at your national shrine. Pray your rosaries for your country to stop its many abortions and its mock-*

ery of my Son's Creation of those souls. Pray also for the sick who come to Lourdes to be healed. When you are healed in this way, it is essential that people's hearts be open in faith and their souls cleansed first. Those with healing gifts should use them at length, otherwise your gift may wane in its effects. In any ways of healing call on my Son's Name and He will hear your prayer."

Later, at Adoration, I could see some clouds and some fighting going on. This was a scene of a spiritual battle. Jesus said: *"My son, you are being challenged in a spiritual battle. Events, as I told you, are speeding up. Your mission has put great demands on your time and your physical stamina. I know you are committed to fight the good fight of faith, but you must adopt other virtues of patience and discernment. Come to Me for your help and I will aid you in difficult situations. You will be faced with many testings in your travel, and even at times your prayer life will be upset. Whatever befalls you, I call on you to treat everyone with kindness and do not let your problems force you to lose your focus on Me. You need My help every day to do My Will. Pray for My blessings to do everything you do lovingly and with My grace of peace. Keep your holy peace at all times, and do not let things disturb you, no matter how much your comfort zone is threatened."*

Wednesday, February 12, 1997: (Ash Wednesday)

After Communion, I could see some candles in a dark place along with some icy flows. Jesus said: *"My people, as you see these pillars of ice in the vision, this is to represent the icy cold hearts of men to My Word and love. I am the Light to dispel the darkness and the warmth to melt men's coldness. As in the Scriptures, now is the acceptable time to come to your salvation. Repent of your sins, My people, and seek Me for the forgiveness of your sins in confession. My sacraments of grace are always awaiting you. You are the ones who must take that forward step to renounce the world and acknowledge your Savior. As you start Lent, let your spiritual walk in sacrifice be a model for your entire life. Carry this Lenten fervor throughout the year. I love you all dearly, especially as My treasured creations in My image. Come, receive your Lord, showing Me your love and your praise."*

Thursday, February 13, 1997:

After Communion, I could see the words *"Choose life"* to emphasize the reading's message. Jesus said: *"My friends, the ashes are over. Now is the time to take up those commitments you have promised to do throughout Lent. The most basic of choices, you will face in life, is your decision whether to follow Me or not. You have free will to reject Me, but you must hear in the reading, that will bring a curse of spiritual death. If you do choose to follow Me, you cannot make light of it on your lips only. In your latest expression, you truly must 'walk the talk' or put into action those beliefs you have accepted. It is not enough to say 'yes, Lord', but you must live the Gospel by loving Me and your neighbor in following My Commandments. You also need to take that extra step in helping others voluntarily, since you can sin by acts of omission as well. I have asked you to do corporal acts of mercy, and it means many times to step beyond your comfort zone in helping with money and your precious time."*

Later, at the prayer group, I could see an old wood burning stove with some baked pies on it. Jesus said: *"My son, be adamant in offering up your gifts of suffering this Lent, so your acts of self-denial will help purify your bodily temptations. Strive to grow in your faith and follow My life in imitation of My ways. Do not pride yourself on any spiritual successes, but give Me thanks and praise."* I could see a large tank of gasoline. Jesus said: *"My people, many of your comforts and your mobility will be tested in the coming days. You will find it difficult to travel as various problems will prevent you from meeting your destinations. Gasoline shortages will return and air travel will be threatened. Do not fear, since you will face many trials. My help will be with you in all of your activities."* I could see some empty sandy beaches. Jesus said: *"My people, many vacations will be curtailed by the weather and other happenings. When you think you can plan your life, many times I step into your life and test you. You need to be purified of your dependence on materialism. It is I you must learn to depend on, for I will be leading you into the world of My new creation. Have faith and trust in Me and you will be led to your salvation."* I could see a bank and there was some kind of a large machine printing out smart cards. Jesus said: *"My people, I have warned you not to take these smart cards, since they will control your buying and selling. Remember, Satan needs electrical devices to control you. Refuse these cards and the mark of the beast, as the Antichrist will use your laziness and convenience to draw you into his clutches of dependence. You will truly be free if you worship only Me and not the world or yourself."* I could see some heart shapes and Jesus said: *"My people, many thoughts of love come with the feast of St. Valentine. It is good for spouses to keep their close bonds of love alive in your acts and communications of care. As you think of your loved ones, keep my love uppermost in your mind as well. Keep your hearts warm in My Presence by your daily prayers. Show Me your faithfulness by following My Will in all you do. Your love for Me will either increase or decrease, depending on how much you enrich our relationship. If you think to do acts of mercy for Me, your love will increase. If you only give Me lip service, your hearts will grow cold. There is no middle ground in My love, it is all consuming."* I could see Our Lady in a statue of the Rosa Mistica. Mary said: *"My dear children, learn the meaning of this devotion, since I am pouring my graces out over all of you in this time of need. I also am adding to this love message for my Son, as our hearts are joined as one. Keep together, my children, in your prayers of love that send bouquets of roses to heaven. See, there are many intentions I wish you to pray for, in helping souls who are in danger of being lost. Pray to save souls from the road to hell."* I could see a barren altar where a tabernacle had been. In place of this was a black velvet holder awaiting some worldly jewelry. Jesus said: *"My people, many have lost a sense of the sacred in My Real Presence in the Host of My Eucharist. You have placed My Tabernacles in out of the way places, since your love for Me is waning. Treasure My Presence, for soon you will find it difficult to find Me in the coming persecution. Then you will see how your preparations for protecting My Eucharist will be made manifest. Your Tabernacle and Monstrance will find its way to secret adoration as Satan's agents will try to strip Me from My Churches. Pray for your strength in those days that you may be kept alive by My special Presence protected by My loved ones."*

Friday, February 14, 1997: (St. Valentine's Day)

At the Tehachapi Chapel, in California, after Communion, I could see Jesus on a cross and there was a bright light about the cross. There were also mountains behind the cross. Jesus said: *"My people, I am showing you the infinite extent of My love for you. Now, I am asking you to have full trust in Me during these end times. You must pray and believe in the signs that I have given you in this place. For those who have faith in My works and protection, I will watch over My people here in this place, which has been consecrated to Me. I love you, My dear friends, and I show that love by providing for all of your needs and your protection from the evil one. Come to this place of holy ground and My angels will watch over you. See this purification as a means to save your souls. You will suffer for a while, but My love will reward you in My time of peace, and later in heaven. Keep faithful in your prayers and I will answer your requests."*

Later, at Los Angeles, California, in a private home, I could see Our Lady of Fatima coming and she was crying for us. Mary said: *"My dear children, pray, pray, pray your three rosaries each day. You must send your many prayers to heaven because your world will soon be on the brink of World War III. Pray for peace in your world, and do not take my request lightly. You must place your prayers before any of your other activities. If there is not enough prayer, you will witness a horrible nuclear destruction, where some nations may be annihilated. Pray for your leaders not to use brinkmanship with the lives of my people. I love all of you, especially on this day of love. I am crying because I do not want to see you fighting in such a destructive manner. Satan wants to cause your deaths. Pray much to frustrate his evil attempts at your destruction."*

Saturday, February 15, 1997:

At St. Mel's Church, in Los Angeles, California, after Communion, I could see a plain cross standing and there were two strings of flowers coming down from the cross. There was a heavenly mist all about the cross. A man was at the foot of the cross. Jesus said: *"My people, in this Lenten season you must come forward to carry your Cross, no matter how heavy it may seem at times. I*

am asking you to come closer to Me in prayer, which is needed now more than ever. You, who are My faithful, should feel it is an honor that you can suffer for My Name's sake. Listen to the words of My Gospel and evangelize My Words to all those with an open heart. You, My son, must never tire in your mission, but you must carry on this battle against evil. Even if you are harassed and persecuted, continue to speak of My Word with the authority given you by the Holy Spirit. 'Go and teach all nations' is My call to save souls, especially in this time of trial. Satan will be strong now, but My grace will go forward in you to fight the evil one. Have faith and trust in Me, and I will lead all of My people, who accept Me as Savior, to a land of milk and honey."

Later, at the Montessori School, in Los Angeles, California, after Communion, I could see Blessed Sister Faustina come dressed in her habit. She looked like a young girl. Blessed Sister Faustina said: *"My children, I am thankful to you for promoting my cause for sainthood. It is Jesus I call all of you to honor and trust. I call on you, my son, to continue in your messages to teach the people to follow my Lord's Divine Will at all times. You have received the message to say my Divine Chaplet every day. You have been faithful in your chaplet. May you make a point in your talks to emphasize the passion of Jesus in this devotion. May you link the following of His Will with living in the Divine Will. I have lived this way by placing this full trust in Jesus. This is how all of the faithful must perfect themselves, by full trust in Jesus and living in the Divine Will. Pray the chaplet often and spread this devotion."*

Sunday, February 16, 1997:

At the Huntridge Theater, Las Vegas, Nevada, after Communion, I could see a desert scene with rocks all around. Jesus said: *"My people, you are seeing this desert scene because many hearts are dry in sin. You are seeing this dry scene also, because you are entering the time of the 'dry' in the tribulation. As I went into the desert to prepare for My death in Jerusalem, so all of My beautiful faithful will be called to witness to Me in the end times. You will be tested and suffer for My sake, but your reward will far outweigh your suffering. Give praise to Me since My triumph will soon come. Pray for strength now since your spiritual stamina must be enhanced with My grace and My help."*

(Miracle of the Eucharist in three pieces joined together) At the Huntridge Theater, Las Vegas, Nevada, before the Blessed Sacrament, I could see a glorious Church that was shining in all kinds of beautiful colors.

This appeared as a celebration of the new Church in heaven on earth. Jesus said: *"My people, I am showing you the Church of heaven, that I am bringing down to the earth. My triumph will usher in a new Church of My making. I will be uniting My people, and bringing them to a beautiful land of my era of peace. You are witnessing the glory of My love as I will reward My faithful with a beauty you will not fully comprehend. My love and peace will so envelop you, that My Presence will seem to consume you. The miracle of the Host is leading you to this new heaven on earth, where you will no longer need Me in the Host. That is because I will then be with you for a thousand years, and you will call on Me in person to visit you often."*

Monday, February 17, 1997:
At St. Joseph's Church, in Las Vegas, Nevada, after Communion, I could see an ark as one that Noah led his family on. Jesus said: *"My people, you are seeing the result of My justice on the people of Noah's time. I am a loving and merciful God, but I am a God of justice as well. I am always open to receive you and I watch over you daily, especially through My angels. Some have a difficult time in believing these events of My purification will happen according to the Bible. Know that what has been written must be fulfilled. Do not feel that because of My goodness, I will not invoke My justice. I am showing you this vision, so*

that you will realize that I am about to end this evil age. I will allow evil as a test for a time, but then My Will will reign with all evil men and evil spirits cast into hell. Believe My glorious heaven on earth is coming sooner that you suspect. Rejoice, My people, for soon you will be in My constant presence in the era of peace. Pray for strength in these days of the trial."

Later, at a private home in Las Vegas, Nevada, after Communion, I saw a mirror on a wall and someone's reflection. Jesus said: *"My people, as you look at the mirror of the vision, you are seeing the reflection of My love in you. See in your free will and spirit that you are made in My image and likeness. As such, you are all precious in My sight in any age of your development. Learn to treasure life, since where ever there is life, I am present by the Holy Spirit. You now see why your abortions are so offensive in My sight, since you are killing My little ones. Reach out in any way possible to protect My babies and keep them from the knife of the evil one. See the preciousness of life and pray for all abortions to stop. If you fail in your efforts to stop these deaths, your country will be liable to punishment from My justice. Pray and never cease praying in this cause. Never cease in the fight for life. Do not let the devil win by your inaction."*

Tuesday, February 18, 1997:

At St. Joseph's Church, Las Vegas, Nevada, after Communion, I could see some tombstones in a graveyard and there were people in wheelchairs. Then I saw a darkness come over the graveyard and a thick mist came over it as well. Jesus said: *"My people, in your Lenten meditations, I place this thought of death before you, so you can examine yourselves more closely. There is a finality to*

ū. m.

death in that after that time, you will no longer have time to wit-
ness to My love. For when you come to the gates of heaven, do not
come with empty hands. During life you will be judged by how
much you loved Me and your neighbor. So go forth and do good
works for your neighbor to store up your heavenly treasures. Also,
take time to show Me in prayer each day how much you love Me,
by following My Will. If you come to heaven with no good works
and you are a stranger to Me, I will say to you, 'out of My sight,
since I do not know you.' But if you see Me frequently, and you
have shown love to your neighbor, I will gladly welcome you into
My banquet. My friends will rejoice with Me, while those against
Me will burn forever in the fires of My wrath."

Wednesday, February 19, 1997:

After Communion, I could see a hill with steps. Jesus said:
"My people, this vision is about the old Tower of Babel, where
man thought he could prove how great he was. It was at that time
that I confused man with various languages. Now, in your day,
man is still showing his pride in technology by all of his elec-
tronic devices. Even as man builds his modern Towers of Babel
in his electronic towers, I will soon confound him again. Those
who think they do not need Me, I will strike their systems and
withdraw their power. By My power I will frustrate man's at-
tempts to raise these things as gods before Me. My chastisements
will come quickly, and soon overtake and dash to pieces any means
to defy Me. Prepare to meet your Creator, since all evil men will
be cast into hell, and all of My faithful will be rewarded."

Thursday, February 20, 1997:

After Communion, I could see a large 'E' for evil. Jesus said:
"My people, you are seeing in this sign of evil, that I am allowing
this height of evil's power to test all of mankind. Look to Me, My
children, as your only hope for enduring this trial. Those, who
choose to fight this spiritual battle alone, will be lost to the de-
mons. Many have refused to believe in Me, since they think they
can do everything on their own without My help. That is why this
test of evil will be beyond their strength, since they will be fight-
ing demons, instead of worldly problems. Rely on My love and

help and I will protect you. See that everything you have and use are gifts from Me. You cannot deny your dependence on Me or you will surely be lost. See that in this battle of good and evil you are either choosing Me or the devil. I hold eternal life for you in the splendor of heaven. The devil can only offer eternal suffering in the flames of hell."

Later, at the prayer group, I could see a ticket counter. Jesus said: *"My son, I have asked you to go public in publishing the messages, and to go out to My people in giving talks. It is important that you keep your fervor in prayer even amidst many trials in your travels. Many souls are being reached, and it is a time to prepare them, since events will take place shortly. Continue in your talks for as long as you are allowed. There will come a time when you will not be able to talk, so go while you can. Speak with the authority of My Holy Spirit, and My Word will touch many hearts."* I could see special marked license plates on cars passing by. Jesus said: *"My people, your car plates will have special electrical devices, so you can be tracked. Only those with the mark of the beast will be able to acquire them. This is another reason why your travel will soon be limited. Know that during the time of the Antichrist, you will be sought out for capture. I will be protecting you in safe places away from these evil men."* I could see an unusual green light which was being caused by the Antichrist. Jesus said: *"My people, you will see strange lights in the sky to indicate the coming into power of the Antichrist. Many will think he is a god to have such power, but in reality these happenings will be caused by skillful illusions. See these things as another sign of power from the man of peace in the Antichrist. No matter how fearsome his powers will appear, I will be watching over you with My arms of love and protection."* I could see Our Lady come, and she was carrying her rosary and scapular. Mary said: *"My dear children, I am asking all of my prayer warriors to be vigilant in their prayers. Pray to save sinners and help those in purgatory. Many prayers are needed at this time, since there will be a renewed power struggle in many communist countries. You could see wars breaking out to fight over food and oil. Continue praying and I will place my mantle over all of my children."* I could see a large disc come in front of the sun as in an eclipse. Jesus said:

"My people, I have told you that there will be many signs in the heavens at the end times. There will be special sightings to announce the coming of the Antichrist. Take care to witness these events, since it will be close to your time to go into hiding. See, I am giving you this information, so I may warn you of these times." I could see a door in a courtroom door being closed. Jesus said: *"Take notice, My people, as your rights will be systematically eliminated. With each decree of your government, you will see less and less of your freedoms, as your privacy will be curtailed and your movements watched. Within a short time evil men will seek to control every facet of your life. As the battle against evil intensifies, you will be avoiding the authorities to avoid capture. I will protect all of those who seek My help as I will strengthen the powers of your guardian angels."* I could see red, blue and yellow colors in connection with the detention centers. Jesus said: *"My people, those, who refuse to work with the Antichrist, will be sought out and placed in detention centers. You are seeing the various colors to indicate the severity of treatment for those who most threaten the Antichrist's power. All those, who give allegiance to God will be outlaws, and the leaders and religious will face the worst of this persecution. Many will be martyred for My Name's sake, but I will protect your souls who are faithful. Be patient but a while, and I will soon strike down these evil men and evil spirits. Pray much, since you will need to strengthen your spiritual stamina."*

Friday, February 21, 1997:

After Communion, I could see an altar in Church and there was a tall wooden statue of Our Lady bowed toward the Blessed Sacrament. Mary said: *"My dear children, I am happy to see all of you that are giving homage to my Son by attending daily Mass. Even though things may get in your way, strive to make Mass and Communion whenever you can. It is being with my Son's Real Presence that strengthens your spirit in the battle against evil. It is as I said at Cana: 'Do whatever he tells you.' I lead you to follow my Son's Will since this is your calling in life. Now, my pilgrims are embarking on a beautiful chance to witness to the messengers being sent to you. Remember, my son, to encourage my three rosaries for peace in your world. Soon events will be drawing you close to the tribulation. Keep focused on a prayerful life and your gifts will continue to bring people to my Son."* (Note: Coming home I saw a white perpendicular cloud in the sky which quickly vanished. This looked like a confirmation of Our Lady.)

Later, I could see a policeman and there was a house on fire behind him. Jesus said: *"My people, I am showing you how many will be tried by vandals and looters in search of food and valuables. They will then set fire to homes they cannot have. Some people will be desperate for their survival and much fighting and chaos will result. There will not be enough police to contain the riots. This is why the people will even accept a tyrant like the Antichrist to restore peace and order. The Antichrist will use these disturbances to take absolute power over many, even over their souls through the mark of the beast. No matter how evil it gets, never seek the Antichrist to gain peace. His peace will be a false peace and your conditions will be worse than when he took power. Follow My protection and I will fulfill your needs. Live for My glory since Satan's power will last but a moment."*

Saturday, February 22, 1997: (Chair of St. Peter)

After Communion, I could see an empty chair as I have seen before representing the pope's exile. Jesus said: *"My son, I have shown you this vision previously about My Pope son, John Paul II being exiled. This is another reminder, but it is also very close. There will indeed be a special election controlled by the evil element of the cardinals. My pope son will be forced out of office and the new false witness will bring a schism into My Church. I am telling My people to follow My traditional teachings and do not listen to the misguiding imposter pope. This false witness will be in league with the Antichrist as a world leader. Evil will have a short reign before I dash all of these leaders to their fall. Have hope that this trial will be brief, for I am guiding My remnant church until the end of time."*

Later, at Adoration, I could see a gold tunnel and a major light at the end of the tunnel. I then could see a bright line of light with ups and downs. Jesus said: *"My people, you are seeing how many will experience My warning in their life review. Everything will glow with My light and mankind will be witnessing the worsening famine. You will learn how much sin offends Me and how you stand so far in My justice. You will have a short time after My warning to convert your lives and seek My forgiveness. Remember to be frequent in your going to confession, so your soul may be found purified. For those seeking to go on your trip, it must be by their own free will that they come. There will always be graces given to those who go on a pilgrimage. Question whether there is more spiritual gain in the pilgrimage or what other devotions and duties you are called to."*

Sunday, February 23, 1997: (Abraham offering Issac, Transfiguration)

After Communion, I could see Jesus with a beautiful face with light all around Him. This quickly turned to an image of Jesus on the shroud. Jesus said: *"My people, I am showing you how I am glorious in heaven, to show you the hope one day of being resurrected with Me forever in My love and peace. For now, you are also seeing Me suffer My crucifixion and death portrayed on the shroud. I am the suffering servant of God who has died for your sins and I still suffer for your ongoing sins, today. Just as Abraham was a man of faith in being willing to sacrifice his only son to God, so I also am God's only Son who has offered My life up for all of you. See My love and dedication to saving all of your souls. It is only your decision to accept Me in love as your Savior and Creator. Commit your life to following Me and you will fulfill your purpose on earth that I have asked of each of you. See your destiny is to share eternal life with Me and come to Me in prayer and good deeds. Wrap yourself in My love and you will see the fulfillment of your soul in sharing My being."*

At Adoration, I could see much destruction and fire that was caused by wars and famine. Many people were looting and setting fires to get food. Jesus said: *"My people, you are witnessing the destruction by the Four Horsemen of the Apocalypse. They will test you with fire, strife, famine and death. Those, who refuse to believe in Me, will suffer the worst in the end. You must suffer persecution for My sake in order to save your souls. Pray for My protection even though this trial will shake your faith. You must seek Me now in earnest. Those, who are complacent and do not seek My help, will be lost to the wiles of the Antichrist. Trust in Me during the tribulation and I will lead you at the time of My triumph. My faithful have nothing to fear with Me at their side. Your reward is not far off, for those who have the patience of faith."*

Monday, February 24, 1997:

At St. John the Baptist Cathedral, San Juan, Puerto Rico, after Communion, I could see Our Lady looking out over a vast crowd. She then appeared wearing a crown and she held the infant Jesus who was wearing a crown also. I then saw the boat leaving from the shore and Our Lady placed her mantle about us. Mary said: *"My dear children, I am grateful for your devotions and I lead you in this procession to my Son in the Mass. Your love for me and my Son always brings tears of joy to my eyes.* (Tears were coming to my eyes as I felt a consuming love by Jesus and Mary.) *I love you, my children, and I do not want to see even one of my faithful ones lost. Keep close to me and my Son in prayer and you will have nothing to fear. Again, I am asking your three rosaries for my special intentions — peace in the world, a stoppage of abortion, and conversion of sinners. See as your trip is starting that I wish to put my mantle of protection around you. Be at peace as a child is held in the arms of a loving mother."*

Tuesday, February 25, 1997:

On the boat, after Communion, I could see Jesus on the cross suffering. Then later, I could see the Host changed into His Body and Blood and there was a sense of a presence in a new world. Jesus said: *"My son, you are seeing Me suffer as you may have to suffer. Offer your suffering up for those souls that may be touched by your words through the Holy Spirit. Even though you may endure trials, I will be at your side to help you. In this opening you are seeing a taste of My real world in the Divine Presence. When you witness to Me in this way, it will be in total peace and total surrender, for this will truly be when you live in My Divine Will. See Me but a moment as I am, so you can witness to others about the glory of My Presence. Live to reign with Me for I am everything your soul is seeking."*

Later, on the ship, before the Blessed Sacrament, I could see flowers from Heaven falling all around the monstrance. Jesus said: *"My people, I am showering all of My faithful with gifts of My graces and My blessings. My mother and I are here for you, always waiting to receive you. When you come before My Blessed Sacrament, drink in My Presence so you can build up your spiritual stamina for these times. Do not ever be fearful, but be joyous to receive Me. I am your refuge and your heavenly food until the end of time. Hold your focus on Me every day and I will guide you to your eternal destination with Me in heaven."*

On the ship, after Communion, I could see a large pool with bars to pull you up. Jesus reached forward a saving arm. Then I saw a troubled sea calmed forever. Jesus said: *"My people, you are awash and drowning in a sea of sin. See, My mercy abounds, as I reach My arm out to pull all those immersed in sin to safety. Seek My forgiveness, no matter how scarlet and crimson red your sins are. I will forgive a penitent sinner and cleanse your souls. Then you will be free once again of Satan's bond and free of his hold on you. Rejoice, My people, for as you will see a great storm of evil for a while, I will again calm the winds and the sea of all evil. Satan will soon be cast into hell with his demons, and I will renew the earth. A great peace and love will come over the earth for a thousand years. The sea of evil will be no more and My triumph will reign supreme."*

Wednesday, February 26, 1997:

At Betania, Venezuela, after Communion, I could see Our Lady come and there were many white rosaries hanging down. I then saw a procession and when it came close, I could see an empty infant basket. Mary said: *"My dear children, listen to your heavenly mother who pleads with you to stop the killing of babies. Hold your rosary in one hand and struggle to save the babies from abortion in the other hand. Your society has become so absorbed in earthly possessions, that you are selling your babies to the doctors for thirty pieces of silver. See that you are betraying my Son again by these sins of murdering the innocent, helpless infants. Wake up, America, and repent, for your judgment time is upon you. If you still refuse to listen to your mother, I will not be able to hold back my Son's hand of justice. Seek my Son's mercy while you can, or many will be cast into the eternal flames of hell. Thank you for responding to my call."*

On the ship, after Communion, I could see the priest reading the Word of God at the pulpit. Then I could see the people being healed. Jesus said: *"My beautiful people, I wish to witness to you about the power of My healing. You know that you are weak in both body and spirit by virtue of Adam's sin. This means you can have diseases of the body and you are susceptible to a sick soul with sin as well. Look to My Death and Resurrection as your strength. Indeed, I offer you a spiritual healing through My sacraments. In order to be healed in My Name, you must be open to the power of My Holy Spirit. He is with you always and all you must do, is call on His power. Listen to the love in My Gospel and you will be open to a loving healing by My Holy Spirit. When your sin has been forgiven, you become a new creation. Once, you are open to My graces, I can raise your being to its full health. Those, who are suffering servants, may continue their suffering. Those others are open to My healing graces. When you seek a healing, it must be in both body and spirit, since the two are joined together while you are alive. See, I work many graces through My faithful witnesses as a testimony to the truth of their faith in healing in My Name and according to My Will. Seek all healings in this manner and many graces of health will be granted you. Remember, it is the spiritual healing that is most important."*

Thursday, February 27, 1997:

On the ship, after Communion, I could see things of glitter and riches. Jesus said: *"My son, you must be open and sharing with all of the things of this life. Do not hold back anything, but be gracious in all you do. Do not be fearful of any repercussion of what you may do. Speak out boldly for Me and spread My Word. Be ready to do corporal acts of mercy at all times. I have taught you before to be more loose with your purse strings. Why are you still restrained at times? You must think to be gracious at all times and not just those that are convenient. Be willing to admit your errors and move forward to change your ways. There are many sins of omission because My people do not have fully open hearts. Do what you can to improve your life in this area."*

Later, on the ship, before the Blessed Sacrament, I could see gold colored strata almost like rocks, only this represented different positions in society. Jesus said: *"My people, why do you look for justice in this world? Many affairs that man conducts are not according to My ways. Yet, for a time I allow the wheat to grow with the tares. There are some who abuse their stations in life to gain riches for themselves. After awhile, they are obsessed to gain even more. But in the end, 'what does it profit a man to gain the whole world and lose his soul?' So do not worry if you will have enough to survive, for the worldly are taken up with these things. Instead, concern yourself with heavenly riches which cannot be taken from you. If you love and serve Me and your fellow man, that will be enough to gain your salvation. I love you so much that I am constantly giving you the ways to perfection. Make the most of your time in a spiritual way and your reward will be great."*

Friday, February 28, 1997:

On the ship, after Communion, I could see many lights as on people of importance. Jesus said: *"My people, in today's readings look at the reason that each person — Joseph, the master's son, and Me — are being rejected. With Joseph, it is jealousy that he is favored by his father over the other brothers. They cannot stand to have someone receive more honor than themselves. Again, in the vineyard the tenant farmers rejected having to share their crops with the owners. It is out of greed that they wanted to keep their crops, and greed also to try and kill the son to inherit the land. With the scribes again, I was a threat to their authority. They are the ones who demanded respect and allegiance from the people. Therefore, take a lesson that you are at ease in accepting authority over you. Do not seek the power of leadership for its own sake. Again, be content with your lot and discard any envy for goods beyond your share. When you seek Me first, all else will be given you. Learn to submit to My Will and heal any of your selfish thoughts."*

On the ship, after Communion, I could see someone who had just received Holy Communion. There was a tingling feeling as Jesus' Real Presence was made known to me. Jesus said: *"My people, I have given My life for all of you that you may be saved*

by My Blood. It is My sacrifice that you renew in an unbloody manner at every Mass. See to it My people that you treasure My Host as your daily bread and My daily Presence that I am offering at every Mass. I love you with such an all consuming love that I wish to envelop every child of mine. See, My children, that you are so dear to Me that I can never turn away your request for help. Come to Me and visit Me often in My Blessed Sacrament. I offered My life freely without restriction that all may have eternal salvation. See My love poured out as a libation for the sins of all men. My blood of forgiveness is upon all who seek it. Join Me in this love of the Spirit which holds your soul in such sweet surrender."

Saturday, March 1, 1997:

On the ship, after Communion, I could see someone washing the floors and then the curtains were opened to a bright light. Jesus said: *"My loving children, it is I, your Jesus, who welcomes you to*

all of My heavenly graces. I have given all of you many gifts, but the most important gift is that of Myself, so your sins may be forgiven. All of you are sinners by your weakness from Adam. It is important that you realize that you are spiritually weak by nature. You need to be praying constantly to be aware of the ways in which you offend Me by your sins. Every day renew your actions and see what you did wrong. Then make reparation and seek confession often to have your sins forgiven. Give thanks to Me for being so merciful in forgiving any of your offenses. Remember, how I have forgiven your worst sins in the past. You may think you are not worthy of being forgiven for these serious offenses, but still they are forgiven. For the one who has been forgiven much, he will be more thankful. I tell you, as in the reading, how heaven rejoices over any repentant sinner. So when you come to Me, seeking My forgiveness of your sins and you are sorry for them, heaven and I will rejoice with you also. Invite all sinners to be forgiven. I will take *anyone back in My graces if they would only admit their errors and be sorry for their sins. See the glorious mercy I pour out on all sinners and give thanks for this magnificent blessing."*

On the ship, after Communion, I sensed a message of suffering as I saw some of the Indian people. (I was a little seasick again.) Jesus said: *"My people, many of you have been severely sick or have had some kind of pain in your life. Your pain always looks the worst until you see someone in worse suffering. I allow suffering to test that soul's faith. For many have come to Me in love through hardship more than through affluence. Offer your suffering with Me on the Cross. I have shown you how to endure suffering. Many progress to great spiritual heights through suffering, as witness to My many saints. See the cleansing power in all that you are asked to endure and do not complain. See this opportunity as a secret blessing for in each acceptance of suffering, you give up your will to Me. Follow My Stations of the Cross, especially in Lent, so you may share in My suffering."*

Sunday, March 2, 1997:

At the Cathedral, at Cartagena, Columbia, after Communion, I could see many of the people's faces crying out for Jesus. Jesus said: *"My people, I am greeting you with all of the loving faces of my local people. See in their faces the love they have for Me and My mother. See that they hunger in faith to be with Me in Holy Communion. It is in this sacred union that your hearts are intimately united with My loving heart. Come to Me, My children, and I will give you My rest. It is the peace of the Spirit that I bring to each of your souls. Know, My faithful, that I am the source of all graces and I give you eternal life. Seek to do My Will and you will be with Me forever."*

On the ship, after Communion, I could see a seat of stability from the motion of the boat. Jesus said: *"Come to Me, My people, especially when you are seeking stability in the midst of turmoil. As you endure your storms of life, look to Me as your anchor who will keep you from drifting away to the evil one. When you are sick physically or spiritually, seek My healing graces which are only a prayer away. I heal all of your problems when you place your trust in My help. No matter how far you wander from Me, look to Me as a beacon who will draw you back. I am always in search of you. Call on My Name and I will be at your side to bring you through any difficulty. With My help, life will be easy for you. On your own, you will be lost without Me. So keep focused on the One you love, and My love will hold you on your course to heaven."*

Monday, March 3, 1997:

On the ship, after Communion, I could see a pathway to Heaven. Jesus said: *"My people, I send you My priests and My messengers to show you the way to your salvation. I have established My priesthood through My sacraments, that through My chosen priests, they may be able to minister to My people. Give thanks and praise to God for the priests who bring My Presence to you in the Mass. Reverence My Presence at all times, since this is how I am presented to you until I come again in glory. Again, I present My messengers and prophets to you in this time to announce My Second Coming and prepare the way as St. John the Baptist did. It is important that the people be drawn to conversion and repent of their sins. You are always seeking forgiveness, but now you will be tested even more by this evil age. I am sending My angels to strengthen you spiritually and protect you from the increasing power of the demons. Fear not,*

since I am watching over you with My words of warning and My power of protection. All of scripture must be fulfilled at this time of My great purification. Heed my words and be constantly on guard as I am coming soon."

Later, on the ship, after Communion, I could see a funeral procession. Jesus said: *"My people, I have gifted all of you with life, but many fail to appreciate a life until it is taken away. Each person you meet should be a joy to experience in this sharing of life. Do not ever take a life for granted, since you do not know how much longer either you or the other person will be alive. Give Me thanks for each day I give you an opportunity to know, love, and serve Me. It will be your service of love to Me and your neighbor that will judge your life. Do not feel a loss in a life that is taken. Think more of the resurrection of a new life with Me. Do not be afraid to die, but see each life is eventually drawn home to Me. It is I who gives life and takes life. Be joyful that your destination is to be with Me in heaven. Sharing in the splendor of My love is your soul's delight. Look forward to and rejoice for the day that you will be with Me in heaven for eternity."*

Tuesday, March 4, 1997:

On the ship, after Communion, I could see a picture of gold or brass fixtures representing the desires of the world. Jesus said: *"My children, you are always seeking to grow close to Me. You must empty your heart of your pride, so you can make room for Me to enter. It is your pride that keeps you from reaching out to help others. It is your pride also that keeps you from seeking forgiveness from others. Make amends with each other even when you must admit that you are wrong. By taking self out of your actions, then you will have Me leading you in all that you do. Look to My leadership even when it is hard and uncomfortable to follow. When you do things selflessly for others, I will be working in your life. Live for love of God and love of neighbor and you will find the pearl of faith you are searching for."*

Later, on the ship, after Communion, I could see a vast crowd on chairs and when I looked closely, they were all unborn babies. Jesus said: *"My people, in the reading the two biggest stars are the unborn babies. St. John the Baptist leapt in the womb of Eliza-*

beth as the announcement of My Presence was made known to him. The unborn are always human and their mothers can never deny the presence of life in their womb. So do not believe anyone denying the right to life of the unborn. The unborn have been given life by Me and their lives cannot be forgotten. See in this huge display of all of your abortions, how many souls that are involved. This is no small problem, but it is a genocide of a holocaust proportion. What is even worse, is that this abomination is allowed to continue unchecked. Do not let Satan control your minds with his death culture. Take your destiny in your hands and fight to stop the killing of babies, the old and souls wishing to commit suicide. If you do nothing to voice your displeasure with this inhumane killing, you are allowing an atmosphere of acceptance and you will be liable at the judgment. Fight for life in prayer and action and you will be following My Will."

Wednesday, March 5, 1997:

At the Church of Our Lady of Fatima in Martinique, after Communion, I could see Mary come in a native dress and she was greeting the people. Mary said: *"My dear children, I am greeting all of you as you come to celebrate with my Son at the mass. See the beautiful souls in all the faces around you. Give praise and glory to my Son for all the gifts of faith that you are witnessing. I am bringing my motherly love to all of you. My Son and I have joined your hearts this day to show how bountifully we wish to shower you with graces and blessings. Keep thoughts of us always in your minds and hearts. We are the spiritual daylight piercing the darkness of sin. See that we are your only hope in these days, and imitate our lives in all you do. We are welcoming all of you to heaven, if you would keep focused on our path to heaven. Shower heaven with your prayers and we will be always watching over you."*

Later, on the ship, at Adoration, I could see the priest hearing confessions. Jesus said: *"My people, why do you not come to Me more often in My Sacrament of Reconciliation? What excuses are you using not to come to Me? Be sorry for your sins and realize that you are a sinner in need of forgiveness. It is very important that you confess your sins personally to the priest in private confession. Without the forgiveness of sins, you cannot enter into the kingdom of heaven. When you commit serious sin, you cut off our love relationship. Your soul becomes dead spiritually and you are unable to have My light in your heart. If you do not come to My healing sacrament, it will allow your heart to be hardened away from Me. In such a state of mortal sin, you will be unable to receive Me in communion or you will commit a sacrilegious communion against Me. You need to renew your spiritual life in confession both for mortal and venial sins. Come at least monthly to keep your soul pleasing to Me. This blessing of a good confession is so important that it will determine whether you wish to be in heaven, or be judged to hell if you do not come. I call on all of My loving children to choose life by seeking forgiveness of their sins. Follow My call to confession or you will die in your sins. Again, I wish to call you out of love, but if it be necessary to call you out of fear of hell, then come. Gain a new, fresh start whenever you receive My reconciliation. See this sacrament as an enlightenment of My graces, for you gain grace with every sacrament received properly."*

Thursday, March 6, 1997:

At St. Peter and Paul Church, St. Thomas Island, after Communion, I could see the people at the hospital being prayed over. Jesus said: *"My son, thank you for reaching out to help My poor little ones in the hospitals and nursing homes. Truly, I have given you gifts of healing which are to be shared. It is an important part of your mission to become part of this healing ministry. You remember in the Gospels how I asked you to visit Me when I was sick or dying. When you do it for the least of My little ones, you are doing it for Me. I will remember you before My Father for all of your kindnesses. Be always willing to pray over My people at any opportunity that I give you. These souls are reaching out to Me for help, and they rejoice at the witness of My love you are sharing with them. Continue to carry on with your mission of evangelization and healing and you will be fulfilling the mission I have given you."*

Later, on the ship, after Communion, I could see a dark stadium with only a few people and some vigil lights. I then saw many people and many lights at some sports event. Jesus said: *"My people, when I return, shall I find any faith in those on the earth? You are being tested by the many gods of the world in sports, money and other gods of materialism. Change your lives, My dear children, so your priorities become more God-centered than self-centered. Do not let Satan and worldly activities distract you from your spiritual goal to follow Me only. Do not let the transitory things of the world which are gone tomorrow, influence you today. Focus your life more on heavenly things that will last forever. I am infinite love. Seek My heavenly love at all times and I will enlighten your heart with a burning desire to seek Me alone over all else."*

Friday, March 7, 1997:

On the ship, after Communion, I could see Our Lady come with her mantle spread over us. Mary said: *"My dear children, I have been watching over all of you with my mantle of protection. When you see me, I am always leading you to my Son. All of you are a witness of my help in all of your activities. See the love of all the beautiful people who have a devotion to me. Many have looked on your group as an inspiration in faith. See by this journey that you are to give witness to my Son and me for all who are willing to listen to our love. It is the love that shines forth from your souls and your hearts that will be instrumental in spreading the Gospel. Your lives should be an example to others of how they can be saved by hope in the salvation of my Son. I love all of you, my children, and I ask all of you to stay close to us in prayer through all of these last days."*

Later, at Adoration, I could see a modern cross and Jesus was being tormented. Jesus said: *"My people, there are elements in My Church who are purposely trying to lessen the reverence for My Blessed Sacrament. Some are even denying the Real Presence in My Host. I tell you, that I am truly Present, no matter how much people are giving Me irreverence. Many are also minimizing the importance of confession and even original sin is being denied. What you are seeing is the growing apostasy in My Church, where My sacraments are being attacked. Satan is trying to divide My church and take away the sense of the sacred.*

The foundations of the Catholic faith are being attacked at its roots and many false witnesses are claiming to be theologians. Many are claiming to be theologians to give themselves authority to tear down My basic traditions. Such evil intended people are trying to destroy My Church from within. Follow the teachings of My pope son, John Paul II and disregard the heresies that are trying to break down My Church. I am with you to the end, so call on Me to discern these false witnesses in prayer."

Saturday, March 8, 1997:

After Communion, I could see a light in the darkness and where sin and evil were evident throughout the world. Jesus said: *"My people, look around your world and see you are in an age of apostasy. I am missing in many lives because man has allowed sin to possess his soul. When people put Me out of their lives, they will reap a whirlwind of destruction, both spiritually and physically. These evil people have hardened their hearts to Me so long that they have forgotten that I exist. You have become perverted harlots in My sight and My justice will rain chastisements against you. My people, many are blinded to My love and mercy by the evil one. Now is the time to awaken all souls and return them to My love or they will be lost forever in the flames of hell. Go out into the byways and hills and shout My Gospel so that all may hear. For if these wicked people will not convert in the face of your evangelization efforts, then they will soon be condemned for all eternity. Teach this lot that their immortal souls are on the verge of being lost forever. Show them that My love seeks everyone, but time is running out for their repentance. If men are not sorry for their sins and they will not seek My forgiveness, then they truly will be accursed and their death will be dark indeed. Pray and wake up to My call or your souls will be suffering forever. Seek My grace and love and your eternal happiness will be assured with Me."*

Later, at Adoration, I could see a head of a cardinal which may represent the newly elected pope. Jesus said: *"My people, the time of the schism in My Church is close at hand. This first beast will also show wonders and marvels to impress people with his leadership. Though he will claim to be a witness to the Coming of*

Christ, he will spew out blasphemies and heresies that will mislead even some of My elect. This false pope will harass My messengers and will attempt to close the apparition sites. See by his coming on the scene that events will happen quickly. For as soon as this religious leader and the Antichrist take power, I will bring My swift sword on their reign. My protection is about all of My faithful and I give you this message of hope that soon My reign will be upon you."

Sunday, March 9, 1997:

After Communion, I could see a darkness and then a cave. Jesus said: *"My people, in today's reading it shows you how I sent prophets and messengers to you out of My mercy before My First Coming. There was a darkness of sin then as there is now. You failed to listen to My Words of warning to reform then and many are not listening to My warnings even now before My Second Coming. Evil has gripped many souls and some are reluctant to seek My light away from their sins. I am pleading now even more that My people wake up from their spiritual slumber. The spiritual lives of many souls are in the balance and many do not understand their destiny is at hand. I call on My messengers to go forward and bring these wayward souls back to Me while they still have time for conversion. Unless these souls follow My Will, they will never see heaven. Guide them to My light or they will be condemned forever in the darkness of their sins."*

67

Later, at Adoration, I could see a serpent laying on a rug. Jesus said: *"My people, more souls go to hell for sins of the flesh than any other sin. All sins involving a violation of the sexual act are mortal in nature and need to be confessed to a priest in private confession. Acts committed by non-married partners are acts of fornication. Violations between other married partners commit adultery. Self-abuse acts are committing masturbation. Any other abnormal sexual acts are also mortal sins. Blocking the means for conception by contraceptives, pills and sterilization are also serious sins against Me. See that all of these sins are derived from a lust for selfish pleasure of the passions. I have given men and women a share in creation of new life, but when it is abused for pleasure only, then you are violating My laws. Since new souls are involved, that is why these are more serious sins against My plan of creation. Follow a chaste life and imitate the examples of the saints, and you will be following My Will. Know that I will forgive you your sins, but you must come to Me in confession. Do not let the body's passions control you, but guard against these temptations with prayer. Give good example to your neighbor in following My Commandments."*

Monday, March 10, 1997:

After Communion, I could see a hippopotamus with its mouth open and it was next to a pier. Jesus said: *"My people, in many affluent places there are areas of abundant food where many times it is wasted. This contrasts to other areas where there are food shortages even causing starvation. Money and power are controlling the food supplies, but soon the famine will upset this delicate balance of life. Those, who wasted food, may soon be found wanting for their own sustenance. These tests of your comfort levels will test your faith and trust in My help. As you lose your own ability to provide for yourself, you will have to call on Me in miraculous ways to protect you. Call on Me at any time, and I will be at your side to answer your requests. Seek Me for your spiritual needs which are more important."*

Later, I could see a large building with shining windows. Mary came and said: *"My dear children, I come to you in many ways — on buildings, in crying statues, on a tilma, in apparitions and many other signs. All of these visitations are gentle reminders of how much heaven is desiring to save the many souls on earth. On pilgrimages, I come with my protection and I share my love with all the beautiful people that you have visited. Continue praying your rosaries for my intentions, and I will guide you along your daily path to heaven. Listen to my messages from the many sources of my visitations. My Son and I are reaching out in love to gather in all the faithful sheep. Rejoice in the loving arms we hold you in. With both of us at your side, your salvation will be assured."*

Tuesday, March 11, 1997:
After Communion, I could see a light reflecting off some flood waters. Jesus said: *"My people, you are witnessing more weather chastisements with this latest round of flooding and tornadoes. Added on to these storms has been a contrived element from weather making machines. Such experimentation by man is enhancing the severity of these storms. Evil men are trying to create crisis situations, so they can cause disruption and destruction of your infrastructures. These same men are trying to establish complete control over the population through emergency situations. Such greed for power through others' misfortunes shows you how devious this breed can be. You will see many controls by your government as they prepare for world control under the coming Antichrist. Do not be surprised that such grabbing for power will confound your land. In the end these men will be brought to their knees as My justice will claim victory over them. Pray for My protection as evil will soon be vanquished by My triumph."*

Later, at Adoration, I could see a house with people doing their chores in the various rooms. Jesus said: *"My people, each day you are tested by many little trials. At times many things seem to go awry for no reason. If you did not get tested, how could you show Me how you can suffer problems and still remain faithful? Pray to Me for help to get you through each day. You need to suffer the valleys in order to appreciate the mountaintop experiences. So do not be dejected over difficulties, but lift up your head in faith and endure each day as a challenge. Have faith in My help and you will be able to overcome any test that may come your way."*

Wednesday, March 12, 1997:

After Communion, there was a bright light eminating from a Host. Jesus said: *"My people, the readings today stress My Divinity from the Father and My love for My people. I came as a man to suffer and die for all of mankind, but remember from whence I came. I am the Eternal Son who came down from heaven to be present with you in human form. My being man does not lessen My Divinity, but shows you how much I love you. So do not let anyone tell you I am not Divine, even when I was on the earth as a God-man. At the same time, I instituted My Eucharistic Presence in the bread during the consecration. Remember to give My Blessed Sacrament reverence, since I am truly present there and Divine as well. Believe that this is how I am still present among you, even to this day in the Blessed Sacrament of the Host. If I were present in bodily form today, you would show Me much reverence. Therefore, continue to visit My Blessed Sacrament and give Me adoration and reverence for My very Presence among you."*

Thursday, March 13, 1997:

After Communion, I could see a large stone plaque as a tombstone or an historical marker. Jesus said: *"My people, there are many sign posts to you in the Scriptures concerning My revelation to man. The Ten Commandments were physical tablets given to man to show you how God wishes you to live. These are today's basis for many of your laws. Another sign post is My Presence on earth which is even related to your calendar years. These are just a few examples to show you the significance of heavenly events on your own history. Look to My life to imitate the way I wish you to follow. Listen to My words of love for God and neighbor. You are given many examples in the saints and prophets I send you. You cannot deny the many interventions in history that I have made, so My Word can be given to all of the people to come to Me. I am forever seeking souls for conversion and My revelation in Scripture has shown you many historical events that have been foretold and have yet to take place."*

Later, at the prayer group, I could see some purple shrouds indicating the Lenten Season. Then I saw Maria Esperanza pray-

ing. I could see St. Joseph with a lily and he said: *"My fellow workers, many of you are forced to work because of the times you live in. Work is an honor for you to fulfill your God-given talents, so treat your work as a blessing and not a drudgery. Pray each day for a pleasant outlook on life, even amidst your daily troubles. If you focus your life on how to please Jesus, then everything you do will take on a new importance."* I could see a green light and an explosion of a nuclear device. There was a strong feeling of hatred emanating from the Mid-East. Jesus said: *"My mother has requested your prayers, especially for peace in the world. Many currents of anger are running deep through Israel and its neighbors. Much hatred is connected with land possession, where each feels they have a right to own the land. Pray, My people, and encourage those parties involved to relax their tensions or war could break out on a larger scale than desired."* I could see Mary crying on her knees pleading for the people to stop their wars and confrontations all over the world. Mary said: *"How many times have I asked you for prayers for peace? My dear children, you are far away from my Son's help in all of your earthly aspirations. You have greed and power always trying to possess you. Do not fall into the many traps of the devil who delights in your killing each other and stirring up hatreds between the people. Come to my Son for His help and seek to make amends with your neighbor. Seek my Son's peace and not the world's peace."* I could see a darkness in a tomb. Jesus said: *"My people, during Lent I am showing you this spiritual tomb, so you can bury all of your hatreds and bad feelings away from you. Do not let petty jealousies and dislikes keep you in an unloving mood. Unleash these shackles which are keeping you from being a joyous, helping person. Start your life anew with Me at the center of your life. I am all-loving, and I wish all of My children would make peace with each other and enjoy the beauty of life in loving each other. Life is too short for you to be sad over any of your shortcomings. Lift up your heads and put My love back into your hearts so everything will be seen in a new light of My glory."* I could see a vision of Jesus suffering on the Cross. Jesus said: *"My friends, as you approach My passion week, I wish you would put aside more time for prayer and meditation on My most precious gift to you — My life. Read the scriptures concerning My suffering and the Old Testament prophesies of how I came to redeem all of mankind. This one act of Mine has changed your lives significantly. You now have the gates of heaven opened to you for those who are worthy. Treasure this true gift of spiritual life which offers a hope to be with Me in heaven."* I could see some cabinets for storing records. Jesus said: *"Lo, My people, I am sending My angels out to mark the faithful on their foreheads and to write their names in My Book of Life. These end days are important in your preparation to face what will come. I have asked you many times to be constantly on guard for you know not the hour of your visitation. Take a lesson from your Lenten devotions of fasting and prayerful meditation. You should be thinking every day how to prepare for your death by keeping yourself holy in following My Will."* I could see St. Therese coming with some flowers. She said: *"My dear children, remember that Jesus said this would be a special Lent. If you have not seriously made any attempts to better yourselves this Lent, then make it a special point to go that extra mile with Jesus. Set more time aside for prayer and time to visit the Blessed Sacrament. Come closer to Jesus in preparation for your coming trials. You will need extra spiritual help, so seek the Lord while He is still near."*

Friday, March 14, 1997:

After Communion, I could see a bullock with horns and it faded away. Jesus said: *"My people, just like the days of Moses when I chastised My people in the desert, today you are still chasing after the golden calf in wanton revelry. Do you expect any less stripes for your actions? In these last days of Lent, look on your life to see how much you are a part of the world. This is a time for conversion and a chance to change your lives and direct them more to Me. Do not be attracted to the pleasures and riches of this life, for these things are passing away. Seek My Kingdom first by following My Commandments, and give your will over to following My ways to heaven. Your soul desires to rest with Me, so shut all of these worldly things out of your life."*

At Adoration, I could see a light come down from the sky and there was a round shaped building over where the One World Religion would be declared. Jesus said: *"My dear people, you are seeing many signs of the Antichrist's coming. I tell you, you will see signs and wonders come about to announce the presence of the evil one, as he takes power over the masses. I will allow a testing time to occur to build up your faith and prepare you to fight the evil spirits. When you see them announcing the one world religion, know these are signs of the coming of the Antichrist. Satan and his agents have prepared for many years, how to take over the world and hold it in their grasp. Be at peace, My children, for I will come to protect you in many miraculous ways. Call on Me and the Holy Spirit to speak out with authority even against your detractors who will try to prove you are false. It is My words that will come from your mouth to confound these people who wish to confront you."*

Saturday, March 15, 1997:

After Communion, I could see a scales of justice. Jesus said: *"My son, go out and preach the words I have given you without worry of what others will say. I will guide your speech by the power of the Holy Spirit. You will face more and more persecution as you bring more souls back to Me. But fear not, I also was persecuted for My mission. The religious authorities declare themselves as the proper authority, but they are the ones in error. Those who teach in My Name, teach with love and not with an accusing finger at every little saying. I was a fulfillment of Scripture, but the scribes and pharisees would not believe it. I tell you, many will come forward to discredit you, to make their own thoughts heard. Do not judge and you will not be judged. Pray for discernment of the spirit and follow My Church. Be careful of the false witnesses who will come to destroy the good work I am doing."*

Sunday, March 16, 1997:

At St. John the Evangelist's Rectory chapel, Susquehanna, Pa., I could see some sea food and then parts falling off an old car. Jesus said: *"My children, you are without food for a short time, and still you seek to be fed. At other times people seek the rich foods, while others are fortunate to have an old car to run. There is little justice in the world of the rich and the poor. When My purification comes, you all will be equally dependent on Me, both the rich and the poor. Prepare now for your surrender of your will to Me. Then when you are tested, you will be able to better endure any hardships."*

At St. John the Evangelist's Church, Susquehanna, Pa., after Communion, I could see sacred vessels which held the sacred hosts and the consecrated wine. They were veiled with a curtain. Jesus said: *"My dear people, come, see the Covenant I have made with you as seen in this vision of My Holy of Holies. I have given up*

My life for you that you may receive eternal life through the for-
giveness of your sins. At the same time, I have instituted My Pres-
ence of My Body and Blood in the bread and wine. This Real
Presence I share with you at every Mass. Receive Me into your
hearts and I will always be with you. Give reverence to My Real
Presence in the way you receive Me and the time you take to
treasure those moments when you share in My intimate love. I
love you My people and I desire to share Myself with you fre-
quently. You must prepare yourself to receive Me properly. Con-
fess your sins in the confessional to the priest before you receive
Me worthily. Never receive Me with serious sin on your soul, or
you will commit a further sin of sacrilege. See by this proper
preparation, you are giving Me the reverence due your Lord and
King. Visit Me often in My Blessed Sacrament to adore Me, and
thank Me for the many gifts I have bestowed upon you."

Later, at Adoration, I could see a cross made out of palms.
Then I saw in another scene a field of crosses that were very numerous. Jesus said: *"My people, I call your attention to your many*
abortions which share their brief life with you. Another facet of
abortion is that very few of the aborted babies are ever baptized.
The reason for this is that most of the mothers do not even want
to recognize there is human life there. I tell you, since the con-
ception of these babies, life can only be instilled by placing the
soul in that single cell. Those having abortions do not even think
there is a soul present. This lack of reverence for a life being
present, weighs heavily on these mothers. By not recognizing life,
they fail to baptize these small babies. Even these mothers I will
forgive their sin if they are sorry for their sin and come to Me for
forgiveness. Encourage all mothers to baptize their infants, so
the baby's original sin can be forgiven. Pray much for these moth-
ers, for their spiritual freedom hangs in the balance."

Monday, March 17, 1997: (St. Patrick's Day)
After Communion, I could see a bishop with his staff. St.
Patrick said: *"My dear son, I wish to thank you for visiting Ire-*
land this past year as I invited you. You are sharing in a mis-
sionary task as I did. It is a great spiritual feeling to witness
souls being saved. Give thanks to the Lord for all the gifts that

He has graced you with. It also places a great responsibility upon you to go out and preach His Word. Continue to witness to Jesus for as long as you can."

Later, at Adoration, I could see a large horizon. Gradually, I could look over it and see a great light shining. In the beam of light I could see a twisted double helix indicating a changing DNA. Jesus said: *"My people, as I gave My apostles a glimpse of My glory in My transfiguration, so now I am showing you through My messengers, how beautiful life will soon be after My triumph over evil. Now you are witnessing an age of darkness because of the influence of evil. A time is coming shortly when My light of knowledge will shine on all of My faithful. This is the light of the new age in your vision. It will be an era of enlightenment where evil will be vanquished and you will be able to make great strides in your perfection. You see by the sign of this new DNA, that your bodies will change and your spirit will be in closer union with Me. You will live longer, but you will still have free will. You will see in this era of peace a true preparation for heaven, for you will be given an opportunity to live in My Divine Will, if you so choose. I will be at your beck and call, and all of your needs will be provided you as in the Garden of Eden. Have hope and faith in Me that those, who follow My Will, will be given this time as a reward for their faithfulness."*

Tuesday, March 18, 1997: (Moses' raises the pole with the snake) After Communion, I could see Jesus suffering on the Cross and there was a blotch of darkness about Him. Jesus said: *"My people, as Moses lifted up the snake on the pole to heal the people, I am lifted up for all of mankind as the healer of souls. For one time, I was made sin by taking on all of the sins of mankind. This is symbolized in the darkness you see over Me. The Father received My Sacrifice as holy and opened the gates of heaven once again. It was this most perfect offering of My life that has redeemed all of mankind. Without the offering of My Blood, there would be no sacrifice. This single saving event has altered all life, since the sin of Adam. I came into the world for this purpose, that I may die for your sins. That is why everyone must come to their salvation through Me. I am the font of grace everyone must* *seek to be saved. Until you accept Me as your Savior, you cannot enter the gates of heaven. I am your passport to eternal life in heaven. Be grateful and give thanks to Me for this saving act of Mine for all men. As you go through the remembrance of My passion and death, look to the day of your own resurrection when I will see you face to face. See that being with Me is the goal of your soul and the only end it was ever created for. Once you understand the plan I have for you to follow, you will desire to follow Me, so you can share eternity with Me in heaven."*

At Adoration, I could see a modern car and there was a light following it. Jesus said: *"My people, in this coming age of the tribulation you will see more and more control of your life by electronics. More cars are being equipped with transponders for toll gates and ways to know where you are. Your privacy will be done away with as more devices are added to your car. Beware of the chips in the cars that allow satellites and helicopters to track you. They even have the ability to stop your car by shutting down the main electronic chip controlling your engine. I mention these things since the Antichrist will be using these means to control you. Know that your travel may be limited by car by all the license gadgets and roads you need special chips to use. I love you, and I will be helping you, despite all of the Antichrist's attempts to run the world."*

Wednesday, March 19, 1997: (St. Joseph's Feast)

After Communion, I could see a vision of the Eiffel Tower in Paris, France which seemed to be an example of man's obsession to build towers. Jesus said: *"My people, for many years man has prided himself with building huge structures as your skyscrapers. In earlier civilizations there were pyramids and other such structures. This pride in building structures was most exemplified in the Tower of Babel. Man was intent on building a tower to heaven. It was on this occasion that I confounded this work with many languages, so they could not understand each other. The lesson for man is humility in accepting My plan for him. When man praises himself as a god and does not think he needs Me, it is at that time man will be brought down by his own errors. It is actually through your own imperfections and weaknesses that*

*you come to know me. I have revealed Myself in Scripture to give
you direction, and I died for your sins so you can enter heaven.
See that your destiny is to return to Me when you die. You are
only tested on earth."*

Thursday, March 20, 1997:

After Communion, I could see a small crude road which looked
like the Via Dolorosa to Calvary. Jesus said: *"My people, as you
look upon the stones of this road, think of the pain I endured carrying My Cross to Calvary. I was already weak from the scourging
and I was forced to carry this heavy Cross of all the sins of mankind. I endured every pain and insult because I had a world to
redeem. I suffered much that the gates of heaven would be opened
for you. Now, in this life it is your turn to suffer for Me. I have led
the way to My Resurrection through My suffering and death on
the Cross. If you wish to be saved, you all must follow Me in suf-*

JOSYP TERELYA   1997

fering by taking up your daily cross and carry it to greet Me. By offering up all of your daily struggles, you are making a prayer and a gift of your life up to Me. Continue along your path of faith in life, and you will be rewarded with your resurrection to heaven."

Later, at the prayer group, I could see several people dressed in dungarees at Sunday Mass. Jesus said: *"My people, when you come to Mass, make a point of giving Me reverence in your dress. You are giving worship to your God and you are not going to a sports event. See also, My people, how a schism is coming in your Church where there are factions not willing to follow My pope son. Follow Pope John Paul II, for he is leading My Remnant Church. You may be forced to go underground in your homes for prayers and Mass."* I could see mothers holding their children and sharing together. Jesus said: *"My people, many mothers are aborting their children for mainly material reasons. For those who bear with difficulties to have their children, they will be given many blessings. Those, who do have abortions, will have to account for their sins. Life is too precious to be discarded, so pray in this fight of good and evil to discourage abortions and to help those in difficulty."* I could see purple garments covering things and representing the coming of Passion Week. Jesus said: *"My people, every year you set aside this special week to honor My passion and death on the Cross. This is a remembrance of My saving act on the Cross for your salvation. Set aside some special time for prayer and meditation this coming week. It is important that you keep your focus on Me at all times in your life. Come, follow Me in the plan I have for all of your lives."* I could see some people traveling by plane. Jesus said: *"My son, I have called you to a demanding mission to spread My Word of the Gospel at every opportunity. You have been gracious to accept going to many places to preach My Name. I have asked you, because time is short and many need to wake up to the battle of evil being waged. Prepare for each place you go to with prayer. Have people praying for this mission and the conversion of souls who will hear your words."* I could see Mary coming and she said: *"My dear children, thank you for coming together to say your rosaries even though circumstances were against you. You must continue to pray together as often as possible. You do not appreciate the power of your prayers said in a group. Continue praying for my intentions to save sinners, to have peace in your world and to stop abortions. With enough prayer you can overcome many evils in your society."* I could see some beautiful Church furniture and some stained glass windows. Jesus said: *"My people, many are trying to preserve the things of the Church. Some are saving old books, monstrances, tabernacles, statues and many other vessels to hold My revelations close to their hearts. Since there will be a great religious persecution, it is important to protect these things from being lost. Look how the church in Russia has been tested, but still the people have a great faith."* I could see a family sitting around the dinner table. Jesus said: *"My dear people, you must preserve the family in your society against all those wishing to tear it apart. Do not let your TV's and excessive activities keep you apart. It is from the family that children draw on the strength of their parents to lead them spiritually. Help each other and see how each of you are gift to each other. You influence others' lives in ways you do not see by your own example. Continue to help form spiritual values for your children and do not give up on them, for deep down they look to you for strength to endure this life."*

Friday, March 21, 1997:

After Communion, I could see some black plastic scanners for reading chips. Jesus said: *"My people, I am warning you once again about your electrical devices, that will be more and more used to control your lives. You will continue to see a wide spread use of the smart cards which I have advised you not to take. The chips on the cards have all the ingredients of the mark that they will try to place in your hand. Trust Me when I am emphasizing how devious these chips can be abused by the Antichrist. You will soon see how helpless you are to do anything without these cards. They will be required at work, to drive on the roads and to buy and sell. But fear not, for I will provide for your needs, so you will survive without these chips. Again, do not take the chip in the hand or you will be led to hell. You have rightly proclaimed this devious plan which is meant to control people. Continue to preach My Word and warn the people to prepare for hiding when the chip in the hand is announced."*

Saturday, March 22, 1997:

At Santa Maria, Calif., at the Cross of Peace, before the Blessed Sacrament, I could see a cross with Jesus on it, but there was a static signal so the vision had lines causing a fuzzy appearance. After the Warning everything became crystal clear and hiding was more understood. Jesus said: *"My people, before My warning there will be some confusion about the events of the tribulation. Many may not understand beforehand the importance of conversion and how their souls are in jeopardy of being lost. My messages have gone out from many sources to prepare for this spiritual battle, but there are many deaf ears. I tell you, after My warning, it will become crystal clear where your allegiances will lie. Those, who continue to love the things of the world, will align themselves with the Antichrist. Those, who see My light through faith and the revelations of the warning, will be drawn to conversion and confession. It will be having your sins forgiven that will set your soul free. Seek to bring souls to Me after the warning even more, for the harvest will be ready as never before. You will have only a short time to save souls, or they will be snatched away by the evil one."*

Later, at Santa Maria, Calif., at the Cross of Peace, after Communion, I could see a new pope on a throne and throngs of people lined the streets. Jesus said: *"My people, I am showing you once again how My Pope John Paul II, will be exiled by a new pope who will assume power. Beware of this new pope, for he will mislead the people. You will see a great schism in My Church where evil will be allowed its day. Pope John Paul II will lead My Remnant Church. Look to the fruits of this new pope, for you will see him violate long standing traditions and dogmas. Eventually, he will even endorse the Antichrist and you will know how evil he will be in all his subtle ways. He is the one who will be slain, but he will rise again from the Antichrist's power. The two beasts will reign but a moment in time, then I will strike them down and My victory will be witnessed. This is the long awaited victory over evil when Satan and the beasts will be chained in hell while My era of peace endures."*

Sunday, March 23, 1997: (Palm Sunday)

At Santa Maria, Calif., at the Cross of Peace, I saw a vision of many seats empty inside the Churches. Jesus said: *"My people, there will come a time at the beginning of the tribulation when no one will be allowed in the churches. At the time of the Antichrist, he will only allow worship of himself. All those, wishing to worship God, will have to go into the fields and woods in secret. The authorities will be persecuting all those with an open worship of God. You will not be allowed to have sacramentals or books that are not approved by the Antichrist's agents. The churches will be used for museums and even black masses. You will be fortunate to find an underground Mass and the priest available. I have asked you to preserve My holy objects for this time when they will be needed. Keep close to My mother and Me through the rosary, and we will protect you from the evil influences. Have hope and trust in Me to lead you through these trials and you will be rewarded for your faithfulness in My era of peace."*

At Santa Maria, Calif., at the Cross of Peace Conference, after Communion, I could see numerous crosses and they were all joined into the shape of one large cross. Next to this cross was a large pool of water. Jesus said: *"My people, look on My Cross in a different light, as you see in this vision. See that all the crosses that you bear in this life are joined in My suffering on the Cross. You are all one body in Me, so that every pain you feel, I feel as well. I have experienced all human suffering, so I know what each of you are going through. Now, as you see the pool of water, see this as My cleansing waters of forgiveness made possible by My death on the Cross. Come to Me, My people, for it is by your own free will that you must seek My forgiveness and be sorry for your sins. You are to sacrifice your will up to Me, so you can fill your heart with My love and follow My Divine Will. I have given you all the gifts necessary for eternal life. Come, share the banquet with your Master."*

Tuesday, March 25, 1997:

After Communion, I could see a negative image of Jesus as on the shroud of Turin. Jesus said: *"My people, this holy week is an important remembrance of My faithfulness to My promise in redeeming mankind. Follow Me by being faithful to My Word in your daily actions. Do not deny Me as in the Gospel where*

Peter and Judas grew weak. Instead, proclaim My Gospel from the rooftops as you are doing in your talks. Remember to keep your focus on Me and you will be strengthened in your spiritual weakness. As you look on the image of all of My suffering, you can understand the extent of My love for you in giving up My life. I share in your life intimately by My Sacramental Presence. Partake in My Sacraments, often for I am reaching out to you in love through them."

Later, at Adoration, I could see a cross with a corpus positioned in the middle of a stage. Jesus said: *"My people, now in these final days of Lent My death on the Cross is taking center stage over all else. In the end it is My love and mercy that will triumph. My death on the Cross is the supreme sacrifice to the Father that has set you free. See in this one act how much I love all of you. The God-man has come into the world, so mankind's salvation may be assured. Without this sacrificial gift, there could be no forgiveness of your sins. Preach 'Christ crucified' wherever you go to evangelize, since it is only the forgiveness of sins that will enable souls to be saved. Come to Me in My Sacrament of Reconciliation to confess your sins and your souls will be set free once again. Pray for all sinners that they may be converted in heart and cleansed in their souls. Many souls are being lost to the evil one because the forgiveness of sins is not being preached. Yet, this is why I came into the world, to die for you, so all could avail themselves of My saving graces.*"

Wednesday, March 26, 1997:

After Communion, I could see a large host being held up at the Consecration. Jesus said: *"My people, I call all of you to My banquet in the breaking of the bread. Through the consecration of the bread and wine, I give you My Body and Blood. Come, share in My Real Presence where I come into your souls to infuse you with My graces through the Sacrament of Holy Communion. This is the true Bread of Life that will last until My Coming again. This is your Daily Bread of strength that I will provide for you even during the tribulation. The angels will provide the heavenly manna much like in the desert. Trust in Me and I will provide your sustenance.*"

Thursday, March 27, 1997: (Holy Thursday)

After Communion, I could see a huge comet and its tail crossed the sky. All at once there was darkness. Jesus said: *"My son, this comet, that you have seen tonight with your own eyes, is the sign of the Antichrist's coming. I have told you before to look to the skies for the signs of things to come. I have also told you that I, and not the Antichrist, would produce this sign of his coming. As you see the darkness come after, you will know his reign will be brief, but darkness will have its day much like the men I allowed to crucify Me for your sake.* (Hale-Bopp comet.)

"At this time, I would like to acknowledge your spiritual director's wish to clarify any reference to a thousand year era of peace. As you know, this reference is mentioned many times in the Scriptures and My references are in the same vain. The leaders of My Church have made binding interpretations of 'millenarianism' which I wish you to acknowledge under obedience to My Magisterium. They have not interpreted one thousand years to be taken literally. I will not reign then in My Body. Only spiritually will I be present. The era of peace will have no evil force, but you all will still be striving to perfect yourselves. Many will have difficulty in understanding this subject, since there is little evidence to make an interpretation about. Suffice it to say now, when that time comes, you will experience the truth as I have willed it."

Friday, March 28, 1997: (Good Friday)

After Communion, I could see Jesus dying on the cross in pain. I then saw a bright light around Jesus in the heavens and all of heaven shared in the victory over sin. Jesus said: *"My people, today, on this remembrance of My death, did your salvation come. All heaven rejoiced at My death, since this was the price to free mankind of his sins. My Spirit illumined the heavens as My earthly journey had achieved My goal to offer sacrifice to the Father for all of mankind. This was the fulfillment of the promise of a Redeemer that would free man of his sins. This giving of My life was justification of the high priest's words that one man should be offered to save the people. When I gave up My life, this was your release of your sins as well. I died once for all men in the past, present, and future. This is why My suffering continues as men are still sinning and they need My reparation. When you pray the Stations of the Cross and honor My death, think of My infinite love, that I would do this even for only one sinner. Join with Me in carrying your crosses and you will one day be rewarded for your faithfulness."*

Saturday, March 29, 1997: (Easter Vigil)
After Communion, I could see Jesus rising from the tomb with His Body and a brightness all around Him. I then saw many souls as spirits rising out of the ground up into Heaven. Jesus said: *"My people, on that first Easter you are seeing how I rose in glory and shattered the shackles of sin and death. Sin and death had no hold on Me, but My Resurrection is a sign for all of you that one day you will be resurrected with Me also. With My triumph over evil, the gates of heaven were opened to all mankind. Those, who were worthy in their individual particular judgments, were allowed to rise to heaven for their heavenly reward. You are seeing all these souls rising to heaven as My death freed them from the bonds of Adam's sin. As one man's sin caused death to the body and spirit, now, one man's death has forgiven all of mankind's sin. Heaven's gates have been opened once again, but it still requires the acceptance of Me by your free will to win heaven."*

Sunday, March 30, 1997: (Easter Sunday)
After Communion, I could see a deep hole in the earth and Jesus arose in glory rising up into the sky. On the one side an angel appeared. Then I could see Jesus in His Body dazzlingly white and His face glowed with golden colors. Jesus said: *"My people, today is a glorious day, since it celebrates My rising in body from the bowels of the earth, where I raised all of those souls worthy of heaven, who died. You are seeing the angels who assisted Me in guiding these souls to welcome them into My glory. This is a day to remember, for it signals the day when you will rise with Me in your own resurrection. My victory over death is your victory as well that you all will share with Me, who are saved. As you view My glorious Resurrection with this burst of brilliant light, you are seeing the glorious new bodies you will have one day. Have*

faith in Me for I will bring about My glory once again when I have triumphed over your current evil age. You will then see My glory with your own eyes and My Will will be made known to you even as you experience My era of peace. Endure this age but a moment until My victory is made manifest. Have hope in Me since you know the battle will be won for you. My power surpasses all evil, since the devil has only been allowed a short time of testing."

Later, at Adoration, I could see a globe of the earth and there were many antennae with a complete network of communication all over the earth. Jesus said: *"My people, I have made you especially aware of the Internet and its ability to control people. Understand also that many of these satellites are in position to make this a long lasting connection. The use of smart cards is being pursued and these cards will be forced on the people with little alternative. These means of buying and selling I have discouraged you from using. You are only a step away from using the mark of the beast chips in your hand, which will be forced on everyone for fear of being put in detention centers. Worshiping the Antichrist will be the price of taking the chip in your hand, so beware of starting with any of these chip devices for buying and selling. Trust in My help to provide for your needs and refuse any such help from the Antichrist who will mislead even some of My elect."*

Monday, March 31, 1997:

After Communion, I could see a small band of Jesus' followers huddled together. Jesus said: *"My people, take a lesson from*

My apostles who were frightened at times and searching for direction. They waited on Me for their marching orders and waited for the coming of the Holy Spirit. During these weeks before Pentecost, you will see your faith summed up for you in the understanding of why I died and was resurrected. I am alive for you and always willing to inspire and bless all of My evangelists. You are called in small groups to go out and preach the glory of My Resurrection and how it should be shouted from the rooftops that I have conquered death and sin. This is a joyful message that all men should rejoice that they are free once again from the bondage of sin and have the gates of heaven open and waiting for them. Accept Me as your Savior and the angels will greet you."

Later, at Adoration, I could see a purple covering being lifted from a statue. Jesus said: *"My people, you have endured your penances and have purified your will through self-denial. Lent is a time to cleanse the soul of all of its bad habits. This purple cloth is to remind you of My passion and death on the Cross. It is an example to you, so you may endure your own sufferings in life. You have been gifted with health and many times you do not appreciate it until you fall ill with some sickness. Offer up all of*

your sufferings and trials to Me, and I will store them in heaven for you. Once you have remembered your improvements in Lent, you can now rejoice in My glorious Resurrection. Your age still has to be cleansed of evil, but I give you hope on that day when all suffering and evil will cease. Continue to spiritually strengthen yourselves in preparation for this final battle with evil. I will be with you through it all. Just reach out and call on Me for help."

Index

Prepare for the Great Tribulation and the Era of Peace

Clinton
  inauguaral address (Jesus)   1/16/97
  removal of opposition (Jesus)   1/9/97
communications
  wire-tapping & TV (Jesus)   1/16/97
confession
  at least monthly (Jesus)   3/5/97
  be prepared to die (Jesus)   1/30/97
  conversion & forgiveness (Jesus)   1/25/97
  renewal of grace (Jesus)   1/23/97
Consecration
  Real Presence (Jesus)   3/26/97
contraception
  sterilization (Jesus)   3/9/97
conversion
  before Second Coming (Jesus)   3/9/97
  change life (Jesus)   3/14/97
  time of judgment (Jesus)   1/6/97
corporal acts of mercy
  hunger and disasters (Jesus)   1/2/97
covenant
  fulfill prophecies (Jesus)   1/27/97
creation
  gift of life (Jesus)   2/10/97
cross
  meditate on Passion (Jesus)   3/13/97
crosses
  sufferings joined (Jesus)   3/23/97
  take up daily (Jesus)   3/20/97
death
  love God & neighbor (Jesus)   2/18/97
desert
  prepare, 'dry' time (Jesus)   2/16/97
detention centers
  Antichrist (Jesus)   3/30/97
  Antichrist control (Jesus)   1/16/97
  colors for treatment (Jesus)   2/20/97
Divine Mercy Chaplet
  passion of Jesus (Bl Faustina)   2/15/97
Divine Will
  home in heaven (Jesus)   1/1/97
  suffering (Jesus)   2/25/97

DNA
  bodies changed (Jesus)   3/17/97
Easter
  victory over death (Jesus)   3/30/97
eclipse
  sign in the heavens (Jesus)   2/20/97
electronics
  helicopters & satellites (Jesus)   3/18/97
empires
  rise and fall (Jesus)   1/30/97
environment
  God's care of the earth (Jesus)   2/6/97
Epiphany
  heavenly gifts (Jesus)   1/5/97
Era of Peace
  coming soon (Jesus)   2/17/97
  end of evil age (Jesus)   2/17/97
  no evil (Jesus)   3/27/97
  preparation for heaven (Jesus)   3/17/97
  purification,original sin (Jesus)   2/2/97
  triumph of Jesus on earth (Jesus)   2/16/97
  vegetation (Jesus)   1/21/97
Eucharist
  true presence (Jesus)   3/12/97
euthansia
  protect all life (Jesus)   1/8/97
evangelists
  waited for Holy Spirit (Jesus)   3/31/97
evangelization
  personal attacks,angels (Jesus)   2/4/97
  time is short (Jesus)   1/14/97
evangelize
  love & forgiveness (Jesus)   1/19/97
  personal responsibility (Jesus)   1/2/97
  preach Christ crucified (Jesus)   3/25/97
  save souls,carry crosses (Jesus)   2/15/97
  short time, confession (Jesus)   2/6/97
  time is running out (Jesus)   3/8/97
  witness the Gospel (Mary)   3/7/97
evil
  battle of good & evil (Jesus)   2/20/97

Lent
  mortify the body (Jesus)   2/10/97
  special preparation (Jesus)   2/6/97
license plates
  tracking devices (Jesus)   2/20/97
Love
  prayer & communication (Jesus)   2/13/97
  study scriptures for Will (Jesus)   1/29/97
manna
  provided by the angels (Jesus)   3/26/97
mark of the beast
  angels and hiding (Jesus)   2/5/97
  Antichrist takeover (Jesus)   2/9/97
  buying & selling (Jesus)   3/30/97
  electrical control (Jesus)   2/13/97
  ready to be deployed (Jesus)   2/3/97
marriage
  vocations, love (Jesus)   2/9/97
martial law
  insurance & federal aid (Jesus)   1/6/97
Mass
  reverence in dress (Jesus)   3/20/97
  sacrifice of Body & Blood (Jesus)   2/28/97
materialism
  be God-centered (Jesus)   3/6/97
  be purified (Jesus)   2/13/97
  decay of our country (Jesus)   1/27/97
Medjugorje
  pray for peace (Mary)   2/6/97
messages
  personal difficulties (Jesus)   1/25/97
  publish & give talks (Jesus)   2/20/97
messengers
  abortions & weather (Jesus)   1/18/97
  witness to messages (Jesus)   1/2/97
Middle-East
  prayers for peace (Jesus)   3/13/97
millenarianism
  clarification (Jesus)   3/27/97
mission
  converson, urgent (St. John Neumann)2/8/97

offer up each day (St. Therese)   1/24/97
  personal difficulties (Jesus)   2/11/97
  personal urgency, omens (Jesus)   1/7/97
  prepare the people (Jesus)   1/18/97
  save souls (Jesus)   2/7/97
  time is short, pray (Jesus)   3/20/97
mortal sin
  sacriligious Communion (Jesus)   3/5/97
Moses
  lifted serpent on a pole (Jesus)   3/18/97
news
  seek heavenly treasures (Jesus)   1/13/97
Noah's time
  justice (Jesus)   2/17/97
one world government
  control food,fuel,money (Jesus)   1/26/97
  control of people (Jesus)   2/5/97
  detention centers (Jesus)   2/3/97
  money, jobs and food (Jesus)   1/20/97
  takeover of U.S. (Jesus)   1/6/97
one world people
  tested and persecuted (Jesus)   2/6/97
One World Religion
  Antichrist's coming (Jesus)   3/14/97
original sin
  baptize infants (Jesus)   3/16/97
Our Lady of Lourdes
  Immaculate Conception (Mary)   2/11/97
parents
  responsibility of children (Jesus)   1/30/97
Passion Week
  prayer and meditation (Jesus)   3/20/97
peace
  change comfortable lives (Mary)   1/2/97
  pray and make amends (Mary)   3/13/97
  pray three rosaries (Mary)   2/21/97
  pray to stop World War III (Jesus)   1/28/97
persecution
  mission (Jesus)   3/15/97
  preserve church things (Jesus)   3/20/97

smart cards
  buying and selling (Jesus) — 2/13/97
  forced on people (Jesus) — 3/30/97
  mark of the beast (Jesus) — 3/21/97
society
  cesspool of evil (Jesus) — 1/11/97
Sodom & Gomorrah
  we are more guilty than (Father) — 1/24/97
Soldiers of Christ
  battle of good & evil (Jesus) — 1/14/97
spiritual life
  permanent relationship (Jesus) — 1/16/97
St. Joseph
  fled to Egypt (Jesus) — 1/9/97
  work is a blessing (St. Joseph) — 3/13/97
St. Patrick
  personal mission (St. Patrick) — 3/17/97
St. Therese
  Lenten preparation (St. Therese) — 3/13/97
statues crying
  signs to save souls (Mary) — 3/10/97
statues weeping
  effects of sin (Mary) — 1/23/97
storms of life
  Jesus is our anchor (Jesus) — 3/2/97
suffering
  a secret blessing (Jesus) — 3/1/97
  offer up, self-denial (Jesus) — 2/13/97
  strengthen for battle (Jesus) — 3/31/97
tabernacle
  lost sense of sacred (Jesus) — 2/13/97
Tehachapi
  place of refuge (Jesus) — 2/14/97
Ten Commandments
  interventions in history (Jesus) — 3/13/97
threats to freedom
  do not bear arms (Jesus) — 2/2/97
Tower of Babel
  pride and humility (Jesus) — 3/19/97
  pride in technology (Jesus) — 2/19/97

travel
  gasoline shortages (Jesus) — 2/13/97
trials
  comfort of God and others (Jesus) — 1/2/97
  tested in suffering (Jesus) — 3/11/97
triumph
  earth cleansed (Jesus) — 1/30/97
  scripture fulfilled (Jesus) — 1/17/97
TV
  events, help neighbor (Jesus) — 1/16/97
UN troops
  moving in USA (Jesus) — 1/30/97
unborn heroes
  Jesus, St. John, Baptist (Jesus) — 3/4/97
United States
  freedoms usurped (Jesus) — 2/9/97
  lost faith,world control (Jesus) — 1/9/97
  destroyed & taken over (Jesus) — 1/23/97
  police state (Jesus) — 1/16/97
visitations
  reach out in love (Mary) — 3/10/97
war
  communist countries (Mary) — 2/20/97
Warning
  glow with light,confession (Jesus) — 2/23/97
  harvest is ready (Jesus) — 3/22/97
  last call, confession (Jesus) — 1/3/97
  purification (Jesus) — 1/17/97
weather
  increased storms (Jesus) — 1/3/97
  more severe,be prayerful (Jesus) — 1/10/97
  record storms (Jesus) — 1/6/97
  weather machines (Jesus) — 3/11/97
weather machines
  control of food (Jesus) — 1/9/97
Will of God
  follow, forgiveness (Jesus) — 2/10/97
World War III
  three rosaries for peace (Mary) — 2/14/97

Prepare for the Great Tribulation and the Era of Peace